Racing Through Life

05/03/17

SBL
£1.00

Please return/renew this item by the last date
above. You can renew on-line at

www.lbhf.gov.uk/libraries

or by phone
0207 361 3610

h&f
putting residents first

Hammersmith & Fulham Libraries

Racing Through Life

A Jump Jockey's Tale

Sam Morshead

RACING POST

Dedication

I would like to dedicate these memoirs to my late wife Sue without whose encouragement they would not have found their way to the printing press.

The right of Sam Morshead to be identified as the author of this work has been asserted by him in accordance with the Copyright, Designs and Patents Act 1988.

First published in Great Britain in 2016 by
Racing Post Books
27 Kingfisher Court, Hambridge Road, Newbury, Berkshire, RG14 5SJ

10 9 8 7 6 5 4 3 2 1

A catalogue record for this book is available from the British Library.

ISBN 978-1-910498-90-3

Cover designed by Nathan Bines
Typeset by J Schwartz & Co

Printed and bound in the UK by CPI Group (UK) Ltd, Croydon, CR0 4YY

www.racingpost.com/shop

Contents

Acknowledgements

MY LATE WIFE Sue pressed upon me that she felt my story was worth the telling. Now that I have told it to the best of my ability, I would very much like to dedicate it to her. I want to thank her for her love, and above all for giving me the confidence to write it all down. It is in fact the story of my racing life so that it therefore does not include much detail of home and family life, and the continuous joys that my three sons have brought me.

I would also like to thank Annabelle and Anthea for all the good times we shared together, and to tell them how much they both contributed to my predominantly happy life. I want to apologise for the hurt I must have caused both them and my children when my marriages broke down. The hurt I felt on our separation was immense but in a strange way merely served to multiply the love I have for my three boys. I want to thank them for supporting me as the chapters of this book began to take shape.

Thank you to all those who have helped in any way either by contributing, or merely for being there as I worked through this tale of the race through my life over hurdles, both emotional and physical. You know who you are, and I will always be grateful to you. Finally, I would like to thank my wonderful stepchildren, Fiona and Andrew who have helped me more than words can say. I may have lost Sue, but I have gained two extraordinary young people who I have come to love very much This is my story and I do hope you enjoy it.

Sam Morshead
St Fillans
July 2016

Playtime

IT WAS AFTER six on a Sunday evening in May 1975. I had had a quiet day after a hectic Saturday at the local Point-to-Point; no winners but two rather hairy rides appeared to have pleased connections, so I was happy enough. It had, however, been a late night, pub supper with my new friends, the now familiar reliving of the afternoon events the day before, good bad and indifferent, followed by a good gas of all the local gossip.

I was full of the joys of spring and the two lots I had to ride that morning did not take long. Without the Guv'nor and only two of us in, tidying up was always a bore but it was fun riding out. Our horses were exercised at the pace we wanted around the farm, but we never larked about over any jumps, although a quick spin and the opportunity to go a bit faster up a nice green grass bank was never missed. If they won the next day we gave ourselves a pat on the back, but if they got beaten there was always another day and surely we could not have done any harm. Our priority was always to get finished as soon as we could. Once tidied, the boss appeared with his cheery smile and he dished out the food into numerous buckets which we carted round to thirty-odd smart, excited thoroughbreds and a couple of not so thoroughbred hunters. Once done, I was summoned into the kitchen, which conveniently opened out onto the yard, to hear tomorrow's plans.

The Whitsun Bank Holiday Monday was one of the most hectic racing days of the year, with nine jumping venues stretching from Cartmel, the tiny picturesque course in the Cumbrian fells in the north, to Newton Abbot near the sun-baked coast of Devon in the south. We were not going that far and had runners nearer to hand at Towcester, one of our local tracks. John Webber, the Guv'nor as we all called him, ran a smooth family operation and was having a good season. His eldest son Anthony, or Ant as he was known, was making his mark as a professional jockey, Ballyrichard Again, The Snipe and others were hitting the headlines on a regular basis, while Theresa his daughter was having a terrific time Point-to-Pointing, with their young brother Paul desperate to leave college to start race riding himself. The gentle guiding light to this successful operation was their mum Diana, who quietly ran the show in the background. 'I want you to ride Hill Leys at Towcester for me tomorrow Sam, and Hugh O'Neill has just rung to ask you to ride one later in the afternoon at Huntingdon. I think you would probably make it but it's up to you.' 'Thank you very much, that sounds great, Hill Leys must have a chance. I hope I can manage to get to Huntingdon to ride the other one, I reckon I will give it a go.'

After this news I went back to my den for some bread and cheese, the bread being rather older than the cheese, which was not ideal, and I fell asleep in my very small

2

caravan in front of the small, old black and white television. Food was not my concern that day as I had been asked by Diana to come into the house for some supper and I also had to do 'light' the next day which was already looking like a red letter one for me.

I had not been in the house long when the phone rang. As in most successful trainers' homes, the phone never stops ringing so I took little notice when the Guv'nor went into the hall to pick it up. It was impossible not to listen and my first impression was that this was not a familiar friend. The Guv'nor obviously knew the caller but by the tone of his voice it was easy to tell that this was business rather than pleasure. The Guv'nor always enjoyed a chat with his owners at any time of the day or night; affable would be an understatement. 'He's riding for me at Towcester then going on to Huntingdon I think, but I suppose we can change our plans if the boy is going to ride a winner for you; I had better pass you over.' My heart jumped, as he had to be talking about me, but who on earth could this be?

'Sam, it's Fred Rimell for you.' From my heart stopping it went into serious overdrive; the leading trainer of the day wanted to speak to me!

'Hello,' I said, rather nervously. 'Fred Rimell here. Where are you going tomorrow lad?' he asked in his strong, authoritative tone. I was relieved to know the answer to that and told him my ambitious plans as if I was doing that sort of thing on a regular basis. 'Well you're not, you're going to Hereford for me where you will ride two winners. My wife Mercy will be there, and she will tell you how to ride them both when you get there; you will see her in the parade ring.' Somewhat in shock I managed to ask what I should say to my owners who had already engaged me. 'Don't worry lad, I will sort that out, be lucky and give me a ring in the evening,' was his brief reply.

I did not sleep well that night, the Guv'nor had been very understanding and was pleased that his protégé had been summoned by the great man, although underneath that happy face I knew there was some disquiet. It was not the first time he had put others before himself. Monday dawned fair, but little did I know that it was going to be the start of a rollercoaster life as a professional jockey that after twelve exciting years I was going to be lucky to walk away from.

An Easy Start

BRIGADIER FOWLER, OR 'the Brig' as he was fondly known, was the first to instil some belief that I was able to ride OK. Tall, six-foot something, straight back, eighteen-inch cane in his left hand, cavalry twill trousers with a heavy crease, he was an imposing figure. 'Sam,' he would bellow in a tone similar to a Sandhurst Guards' parade, 'bring yourself here.' I would trot my precious little pony, Tonka, a rich bay Connemara cross, up to him and look forward to the opportunity to complete his instructions with a broad grin on my face. If he wanted something done it would always test my limited ability, but it would be fun and a challenge not to be turned down. We did all our riding on the sands at our Pony Club Camp, not far from where the famous Laytown races are held. We only lived two miles down the same strip of sandy coastline situated on the east coast of Ireland, twenty miles north of Dublin.

Great big bell tents were our homes for the week – boys' and girls' tents separated by two large marquees where the helpers slept, cooked and generally kept a sharp eye on our whereabouts. They were happy days, riding on the beach by day, spin the bottle every evening and wakened bleary-eyed each morning by a large, heavy brass bell and the cries of 'Wakey wakey, rise and shine, meet the early dawn.' Our precious ponies were kept in a large field adjacent to the tents and caught before breakfast to be tied to a post and rope quadrangle, ready for grooming, never my favourite pastime, before we set off in various age groups to improve our riding and have fun.

My pony at the time was a star; he was small but quite fast with a good jump in him. We had enjoyed some great days with the Louth foxhounds and the local harrier pack during the winter and I was already looking forward to more when winter came around again. We all lived for our hunting. Mum and Dad had always managed to ensure that my elder sister Lucy, brother Hugh and I each had a pony that could keep up with the hounds. Through a fence, over a fence, round a fence, it did not matter provided we were all there at the end.

Mum and Dad both went well and the week ahead was planned around the most suitable meets which very often meant an hour and a half in the car before we could unbox for eleven. Many times we were dropped off some distance from the meet for Mum or Dad to turn round and go back for the second lot. Dad could not always be there as he had to go to his office in Dublin, but he never missed a Saturday and would often escape for a Tuesday meet of the Wards to chase the carted deer. It was always a standing joke in his office that on a Tuesday he would have his hunting clothes on under his office suit and would be taking a long lunch and Mum would have both their horses ready for the meet at 1pm. From Cornish roots they had moved to Ireland to enjoy the hunting and the fishing. I had a lot to be grateful for.

I was sent over to England to Twyford Preparatory School at the tender age of eight knowing more Latin than English – my father had insisted on teaching me amo, amas, amat and a little bit more, while I had not grasped much written English in my school in Drogheda, which was not a good start to my formal education. My brother and I were meant to go on to Winchester, but thankfully we avoided that thanks to a common sense approach by my father, rather than trying to ensure we aspired to his own achievements there forty years earlier. St Columba's College, perched on the northern slopes of the Wicklow Hills overlooking Dublin, welcomed me in the autumn of '68. Black gowns, soon cut short to hang just over the shoulders, took some getting used to. Thankfully, as I had come from England, I was spared the necessity of learning Irish and muddled through with some happy memories on the sports field, without which I am not sure I would have survived at all.

One winter's morning, on the way home for a much needed Sunday lunch, Dad turned right rather than left only five miles from home and said he needed to look at a horse. I remember the setting of a rough old line of boxes with a cobbled yard and red stable doors that had not seen a paintbrush for many a year, with a dozen fresh, keen faces all looking out expecting food. We were shown into a small box which was filled by a not over-big, kind-looking racehorse. He must be a racehorse, I thought, as he is narrow and has thin legs. I did not know much about horses, although I should have done. The tendon on his off fore was, however, thinner than the other, and we were soon to be informed that he had suffered a tendon injury and had broken down more than once. My father was informed that due to his bad legs, this one was off to the knacker's yard but he could have him for £100 if he wished. I remember him feeling his legs quite a few times showing his obvious concern about his swollen tendon, but then uttering the magic words, 'We'll have him.' As we left, Dad said with great pride, 'You boys will win some Point-to-Points with him, mark my words.' Top Up was home in our small yard of three hunters on Bellewstown Hill within twenty-four hours.

The previous year my brother Hugh had won the Little Mares Grand National on my father's Bronte's Cottage at the Shillelagh Point-to-Point deep down in Wicklow. At seventeen I was now ready to try to follow in his footsteps. However, my first ride on Bronte ended in a heavy fall; I was on the inside and did not give the little mare enough light and we crashed unceremoniously to the ground. Dad was not pleased. Top Up had benefited from endless care and attention, including some home brew and plenty of eggs in his weekly mash, and he was now pleasing Dad at home, so hopes were high when I took a day off college and set off for the Kildare Point-to-Point at Punchestown. I was a kid in a man's world, but I had a horse and once on board the opposition meant little to me. Top Up was a good 'un and won by a length or two. Dad was proud, Mum was relieved and I went back to school thinking all this was fairly normal. We won next time out as well at Baldoyle on the old racecourse site. The Louth Hunt Cup was smuggled home in a large paper bag from Quinnsworth supermarket and plans were made for Top Up to hit the big time.

The Irish Grand National meeting at Fairyhouse came and went with a swirl. Top Up won the Joseph O'Reilly Memorial Cup Hunters Steeplechase over the Irish Grand National course, my first ride over the big fences. The cup was huge, the achievement was as big and I went along with the flow. Exams came and went, and dreams of university faded fast with my father's words, 'We have given you the best education we could afford, the world is now your oyster,' ringing in my ears. I was on my way into the fast lane on a 50cc Yamaha motorcycle to work for John Fowler, son of my tutor ten years earlier, the Brigadier.

Rahinston House, situated in the heart of County Meath, was huge and the Brig still had his eighteen-inch cane in his hand, but I was welcomed into the family fold and given a large bedroom at the back of the house. I was there to ride horses and that is what I did, all morning and some of the afternoon, day in, day out and for the first time I got paid for my efforts. Not that I deserved much. Paddy the head lad, with a permanent twinkle in his eye, invariably tacked up my horses and Billy, always with a tale to tell or a fox to hunt, helped me all the way. I was having fun but whether I was learning enough, time would tell. The Brigadier was always at hand demonstrating riding skills that I would never aspire to. I went home every weekend with corn in my pocket to drop off by the roadside in the woods with the aim of nailing a pheasant or two on the way back with the front wheel of my nifty fifty. It was a challenge that provided Billy and me with continual entertainment through the winter, but not often did we have run-down pheasant for our supper.

My first experience of schooling over hurdles was not far around the corner and Strange Delight was suitably named for the purpose. He was on the small side, the wing of the hurdle was on the tall side and we went out underneath. With only a cloth cap on, it meant a visit to the local hospital as, of course, we had chosen to push through directly under a protruding nail. A white gauze similar to an Indian turban was my headgear for a week or two. I had also been schooling the Brigadier's own mare Coppaleen, and as soon as my head had healed she was due to run at Wexford, a tight little track down south. 'Sam, you will ride her and she'll win!' I was very excited as Coppaleen had schooled well and wouldn't have blown a candle out when we went right round the big field in front of the huge historic house, avoiding specimen oaks as we went.

It was a long drive down to Wexford. Billy was at the wheel, the Brigadier in the front seat and I sat quietly in the back trying not to get car sick. Billy came with me to the changing room and thankfully I found the same valet, Tom Fox, that I had at Fairyhouse. I do not remember what instructions the Brigadier gave me, probably just, 'Go out there and come back first, Sam.' He was never one to beat around the bush. Knowing the shortest way around a circle is round the inside I went that way. Coppaleen never put a foot wrong as she jumped like a buck and won at a reported 200/1 on the Tote. Paddy and Billy had made a few bob; the Brig had backed her too so waking up next morning I had a smile on my face.

That smile did not last very long as a week or two later, when riding little Strange Delight at Fairyhouse, I heard Bobby Coonan, a great jockey and one of the hard men of the day shout over to John my boss, 'John, do you fancy your other one?' John innocently replied, 'No, just having a run, Bobby.' With that Bobby shouts over to Tommy Murphy, another top-flight hard man of the weighing room: 'Come on Tommy, we'll teach young Sam while we have the chance,' and with that they came at me from both sides bringing me to a near halt in no more than six frightening strides. A happy run around enjoying a nice leap or two from Strange Delight turned into a hard lesson on the rules of race riding. My innocence at Wexford had not gone unnoticed; you should not go up the inside, as overtaking on the racecourse on the inside could cause road rage!

Still in a bit of shock in the jockeys' changing room afterwards, I got a friendly hand on the shoulder from Mr Coonan who told me with a big grin on his face that it was a lesson that I was best to learn early in my career. I certainly knew from that day on I should never pass these guys on the inside and certainly not when they are fancied. It was a good lesson and the inside rail became a special place for me in the years ahead.

Thankfully I was often lucky enough to be riding horses good enough to take advantage of that position and keep the gate closed if someone tried to break that unwritten rule. Unfortunately, three years later I was to break this unwritten rule with devastating consequences. I was also to try to enforce it at a particularly bad moment at the Cheltenham Festival, not out of harm's way like Messrs Coonan and Murphy, and paid the highest price, a five-day ban from the stewards. I was, however, now really getting the bug of this race riding lark. I was riding much shorter, probably too short, but I was loving the speed, the flying birch and mud and the raw competitive battle of every race I was fortunate enough to take part in.

A Steep Learning Curve

WITH SUMMER APPROACHING, the horses at Rahinston were now due a rest with their reward being the best of the early summer grass. With less horses to exercise there was not enough for me to help with, so John kindly found a place for me at one of Ireland's leading dual purpose yards of the day – as indeed it still is now – Edward O'Grady's, deep down in South Tipperary. This was a different kettle of fish to the rather cosy spoilt existence I had had before; this was a survival of the fittest and I had to knuckle down to some hard work. Sixty-plus horses, most of them during the summer being smart two- and three-year-olds to run on the Flat, and twenty or so lads.

Tim Finn was head lad and Michael 'Mouse' Morris was stable jockey. I was at the bottom of the pile and often reminded of that either due to my lack of experience or to ensure I was kept in the right place. I could have helped myself more by not asking to go on our annual family fishing holiday two weeks after arriving to work, but fishing was my passion and I had not accepted as yet that I had just started my working life proper. While away in the west of Ireland I did manage to buy my first car, a grey mini pick-up for £110. She was no beauty but she turned out to be a great little goer and gave me the wheels I badly needed.

Tim Finn, a man with a wealth of experience and more stories than Dick Francis, did at times get fairly exasperated with me. 'Do you think you are driving a bloody car,' he shouted one morning as I was trying to do my best to ride with my reins bridged for the first time. Next time I passed him on the sand circuit he roared, 'Did you ever see Lester Piggott hold his reins like that you idiot?' Exasperated he might have been but there was plenty of humour in his voice. I was learning the hard way. I had managed to ride two Point-to-Point winners and two under rules without knowing very much; to survive in this yard I was going to have to learn fast. I was never looking more than a week or two ahead; after all this was not going to be my career, I just needed to survive with my pride intact.

I had not been there very long when a nice young chestnut gelding arrived in the yard, another new horse, nothing special about him, just one more to look after. But we all soon realised there was something special about this one. He was given the name of Moneyspinner and, after only a couple of weeks, he was working with some of the best horses in the yard. To my surprise I was asked to school him – he was the proverbial natural. Then all of a sudden one Saturday morning his box was empty and he was gone. Tim had not turned up for work either, which was almost unheard of. Tom Busteed, the senior amateur in the yard at the time, went and saw Edward and was told that Tim had the weekend off and the horse had gone home. We might have been green but we were not that green. This horse was being set up for a gamble and we were not going to miss out.

Quite a few of the lads liked a bet, and one lad who had been at O'Grady's some time, John St John, was determined to get to the bottom of this. He knew that Moneyspinner was a four-year-old gelding by Arctic Slave, so we all scanned the papers for a chestnut gelding running that Saturday afternoon by Arctic Slave. Eventually one was found in a Maiden Hurdle at Wexford, which looked perfect. John collected all our hard-earned cash and off to Wexford he went. The afternoon, like many, was spent playing pool in the local pub, but we were not concentrating much on the pool when the result of the 4:30 at Wexford was due on the transistor radio. Our horse was nowhere. Great gloom descended, as most of us had sent far more than we could afford to lose down to Wexford to ride on this certainty. We were still playing pool when John reappeared an hour later. What is more, much to our annoyance, he had a great big grin on his face when he poked his head around the door. 'What are you smiling about you plonker?' or, in some cases, stronger abuse rained down on him as he entered our den. 'It was not the right horse, I spotted it right away, so believe it or not I did not put any money on it!'

So after all that we got our money back, much to my relief – I hated losing money. There were not many flies on John St John. Sunday came and went, no sign of Moneyspinner and Tim was still away. Monday, back to the old routine and we had too many horses to muck out and a long morning ahead. On Tuesday morning we were preparing ourselves for action with a quick cup of tea and checking out the English results in the *Sporting Life,* when Tom exclaimed with more than a little excitement in his voice, 'Bloody hell boys, Timmy Jones won a race at the Cartmel Bank Holiday meeting yesterday and guess what, it was a chestnut gelding by Arctic Slave by the name of Gay Future.' A collective sigh went round the room. We had missed the sod after all. However, little did we know the fun was far from over.

Day by day the story of the epic gamble began to seep through the yard. Tales of Tim Finn rubbing soap all over the precious Moneyspinner or Gay Future before he was exposed to the big holiday crowd at Cartmel to give the impression that any chance this single Irish runner had was sweated away in the preliminaries. Tim himself was dressed far from his usual immaculate turn-out and when Timmy Jones, the most professional of any amateur of his day, got on with his leathers longer than John Wayne chasing Indians across the Midwest, the scene was set for one of racing's great gambles and no one at the races that day was going to wager even a small interest in Gay Future. That was indeed one of the many ploys in this subtle sting. The price that Gay Future started that afternoon was going to be crucial to the end payout, so this important part of the plan worked to perfection as Gay Future drifted in the betting.

Unknown to the bookmakers standing at Cartmel, money was, however, quietly being distributed in small amounts throughout Ireland and indeed in betting shops in the south of England, and particularly in a mass of London shops. The second vital element of the plan was the choice of Cartmel as the venue for this coup. It was well before the days of mobile phones and Cartmel had no telephone connection at all to or from the betting ring. Word of money in the high street betting shops on Gay Future could not therefore be relayed back to the course to shorten the starting price. It would have been very unlikely that any strange betting patterns would have been noticed as the numerous small bets had been placed not on Gay Future to win, as this might have caused the alarm bells to ring; most, if not all of the money, was on doubles and trebles with two other horses. Here lies the third and perhaps most notorious part of the sting – the other two horses, although declared to run in the morning papers, were never going to get as far as the races that afternoon. Therefore, all this money was riding on Gay Future to win, and win he did. Once at the start, Timmy Jones pulled his leathers up and his goggles down, rode like the semi-professional he was and Gay Future, racing near the front jumping impeccably, bolted in unchallenged. The coup was landed successfully and more than one champagne cork was popped in the south of Ireland that evening.

It was only beers we were drinking in the hotel in Killenaule some three weeks later. Tom Busteed and I had been joined at O'Grady's by a very fresh-faced Niall 'Boots' Madden. We sat on high stools – we needed them – making half a pint last much longer than it should, when in walked Ireland's answer to The Sweeney. Long

Mackintosh, trilby on one side of his head, slight droop of the left shoulder. He bought himself a drink and after no more than a leisurely sip he manoeuvred himself over to our end of the bar and smoothly got us all talking about racing. Some mug punter wanting info was our first impression, knowing as little as we did we felt privileged to be asked. After about ten minutes of talking about some of the stars in the yard, without warning Tom, who was far more switched on than myself and Boots, kicked me on the shin and whispered, 'Gay Future, he's a cop, say nothing.' To our amusement we had indeed been told to say nothing by Edward soon after the coup hit the newspapers, but we never expected to have the opportunity, even if we did know anything about it. Boots, however, was a great one to talk, even at that very early stage of his career, and he sang away like a goldfinch chewing thistledown, telling our new-found friend how smart this Arctic Slave four-year-old was at home and how beautifully he jumped. All Tom and I could do was give him a thick ear once we had escaped from the clutches of this London bobby, but as none of us knew any of the detail, all three of us could have sung all night without giving any of the plot away. We were just aggrieved not to have been able to take the opportunity to line our own pockets with silver.

The monotonous mornings of muck, sweat and aching muscles, and being sworn at quite a lot, were proving a test to my commitment to a future in this game. But I got a buzz from the riding and the team spirit in the yard meant we joined in the excitement as more and more horses began to take their chance on the racetrack. However, I still needed a break from it and, after an arduous morning, I often escaped with my fishing rod to chase trout in some of the rich Tipperary trout streams. I enjoyed the added incentive of bringing fresh trout back to Mary, my boss's mother, with whom I had digs at the time. Fun and success means little if you cannot share it and Mary loved to be presented with a nice fat brown trout for her tea.

On one summer afternoon seeking both solitude and fish, to my surprise and amusement I walked straight into a couple smooching right down the bottom of a leafy lane beside the river. They were huddled in the back of an old car I knew well from the yard; it was Tim Finn's and he was with Edward's secretary at the time. Fish were not the only thing I was catching that day and when I got home I got the definite impression that my landlady enjoyed this tale rather more than the trout we had for supper that evening. I was too green to realise the significance of it at the time, so I have no doubt the loving couple suffered far more anguish than was necessary. There was perhaps another lesson in this encounter that I failed to grasp.

I don't think it was anything to do with this secret that I had inadvertently found out but soon I was being put on some pretty awkward animals and what ability I had was being tested to the full. Many a morning my arms were being stretched to the limit but the disgrace of being seen to be run away with got me through without disaster most of the time. Very very occasionally Edward would

19

let me ride one on the racecourse for him. Nearly all of these were there for the education; both young horse and rider were learning together. I was being allowed to school fairly regularly, and as winter approached there were a lot of horses to school. Mouse came over a bit but often it was the Hanley brothers, Tom Busteed and myself. We went some gallop over fairly flimsy flights of old hurdles; the gentle pace of Fowler's was long gone and this was a hard school. I learnt that horses were there to do a job – Edward could train them and Mouse could win on them when required. They were a hard team to beat when the money was down and I was a very long way down the pecking order.

One of the hooligans I had to ride every morning was a black mare called Commeragh Vision. Every time you got near the gallops she would get into a frenzy, fly-jump like a cat on hot bricks and then take off. 'You can ride her at Clonmel next week,' Edward told me. Doomed to a disgraceful runaway in public was not an unrealistic fear. I remember little of the day – perhaps nerves got the better of me – and I found some extra strength, the wild mare behaved and we won with something in hand. My first ride over fences had been a winner, my first ride over hurdles was a winner and now my first ride on the Flat was a winner, so I was delighted. By the look of the owners and Edward's face when I came back to the winner's enclosure it was not, however, the expected result and Commeragh Vision left the yard the next day. I was never told what the problem was but I know that I did not get my palm crossed with silver for my win. It was not going to be the only time I appeared to be in trouble for winning a race.

Soon after this I might have been one of the most unpopular amateur jockeys in Ireland if I had managed to win a small amateur handicap hurdle at Bellewstown in June 1975. I had been asked to ride Glenallen for Robin Kidd who trained a small string at Loughbrickland in Northern Ireland. He told me the mare might start at long odds but as there was nothing with any form in the race she had a good chance, so they were going to try for a small gamble and would be backing her both to win and be placed. Little did we know that one of the great gambles of Irish racing, if not the greatest, was being planned on Barney Curley's Yellow Sam, ridden by Michael Furlong.

Glenallen started at 12/1 in recognition of those small each-way bets. There was no interest for Yellow Sam on course and he was due to start at 20/1. I thought I rode a good enough race and Michael and I were upsides at the last. I am not sure how much of a fright we gave them but Yellow Sam did go on and win by a length and a half. We were delighted with our run but nothing like as happy as Barney Curley as he won a reported £300,000, equivalent to £1.7m today when adjusted for inflation. The same ploy that the Gay Future coup had used was a vital element to this gamble. The only two telephones on the course at Bellewstown were continually blocked by Barney Curley's team so that word of any money being bet on Yellow Sam around the country could not get back to the course in order to reduce Yellow Sam's starting

price. Little did I realise at the time but riding successfully for Robin Kidd was going to provide a life-changing
moment eleven months later for me as his brother Jack
was travelling head lad to Fred Rimell and these two
brothers must have discussed Glenallen's good run and
her young inexperienced pilot.

The Bigger Playing Fields of England

MY FATHER, ALTHOUGH office bound, was a sports-man at heart and was watching my progress with more interest than I had realised. He liked the hard school and had brought my brother and me up to be tough, well-mannered and independent. He showed little obvious emotion but deep down there was more passion, honesty and courage than anyone I knew. He saw that his young-est was still bouncing like the proverbial cork in a storm and thought a change would be a good move. Plans were made, unbeknown to me, to further my education and ex-perience across the water. It turned out to be a wise move, but perhaps the timing was not ideal as, looking back, the time was right for me to take a pull and enjoy some time at home to lap up some of the knowledge hidden within a lifetime full of rich experiences before my dear father passed on to another happy hunting ground. Another op-portunity to learn was passing by.

The grey mini pick-up and I, laden with no more than a suitcase, took the route that thousands of Irishmen had taken in the past – the ferry from Dublin to Holyhead. The difference was I was not going to chase my fortune and I was lucky enough to know where I was going; unlike many before me, this was just an adventure for me. I felt I had done okay so far. A few Point-to-Point winners and three winners under rules with a few placed runs to add to the experience, and I felt I was now ready to take the opportunity to push open a few doors and see if by chance a career would unfold worthy of my expensive education. I enjoyed riding horses and the chance to do that on the bigger playing fields of England filled me with excitement; another year of fun with no great expectations.

I took the winding A5 like so many before me and somehow I found my way to Cropredy Lawn Farmhouse in the heart of Oxfordshire. I had been warned that home was going to be a caravan, so that was no surprise; although smaller than expected that was not a problem. It was dry and I had all I needed – a bed, a telly and a small cooker. The yard was immaculate, the tack appeared almost new compared to what I had been used to at O'Grady's. Above all else I was walking into a happy team, and things were definitely looking up. John Webber was a big man with a rosy face and he was enjoying a good season. Farmer first and foremost and a keen hunting man, training a string of quality jumpers in the heart of the Oxfordshire countryside had progressed in a relatively short time from a few Point-to-Pointers for the family to enjoy, to interest and investment from friends and colleagues, and in five short years his horses were taking up as much time for him as his productive farm. There was the added incentive that his eldest son, Anthony, had turned professional two years earlier, so every runner, let alone every winner, put a little jam on the family's toast. Like many before him Anthony had realised if you are going to risk body and mind on a regular basis you might as well get paid for it.

I was not risking body and mind very often on the racetrack and was dying to do more. The first chance came with one, Hill Leys, for the Guv'nor at Towcester. It ran well and finished second but the lasting significance of that visit to the races was that at the door to the jockeys' changing room I was greeted by Master Valet John Buckingham of Foinavon fame. He had been warned and he took my bag and put me in his section of the changing room. Competition for the new recruits was fierce among the valets and unbeknown to me I was going to have many happy years with John and his brother Tom. They were both going to play a critical role as my career; many a time they saved me from destruction and disaster.

From that first ride things progressed as a few outside rides came along, and for the first time I had some cash in my pocket. I needed a bit as my wheels and I had a brief encounter with Banbury police who found many of the essentials on my precious mini were not working. The Point-to-Point season was just getting underway, so my mini and I dashed about schooling whenever there was half a chance and I jumped on all the spare rides that were going. Somewhere at some stage that spring, Fred Rimell's travelling head lad had spotted me at the races, remembering his conversation with his brother Robin some nine months earlier, so when Fred, in desperation to find a jockey for two of his six runners the following day, asked Jack if he knew of anyone who might be available, he advised in his quiet Irish brogue, 'Here's one for ya, ring John Webber and get hold of young Sam, he will do the job for us.'

There was a lot of chat in the Webber household that night, with young Sam off to ride for the Rimells – what a to-do! The Guv'nor was wise and thoughtful: 'An opportunity many would cry out for, but mind you watch out for Fred's good wife Mercy, she'll put you in your place, a fearsome woman.' I was never very good with 'fearsome women', and my small supper began to look very big on my plate. Thankfully Theresa saw the whole thing as the makings of a good joke and couldn't wait for my return from this baptism of fire, with Anthony pushing an equally light supper round his plate while good-humouredly muttering, 'Lucky sod, you have more chance of riding a winner than me!' Winners, winners, winners – it was all about riding and training winners; well to everyone else that seemed to be the case, so I thought I had better follow suit.

My stomach leapt into action on picking up the *Sporting Life* the next morning when I saw my name up against the two Rimell runners at Hereford. It did a half-somersault and flip with backward twist when I saw they were both favourite. I was oblivious to the goings-on in the yard that morning, hectic as undoubtedly it was, as my mind was elsewhere. Riding two winners was not only expected but a real possibility and on top of that I had to cope with Mercy Rimell. Youthful confidence ensured that riding the horses did not concern me much but she was an unknown factor, and the unknown has always given me problems.

Theresa and I had become good mates and, a mixture of worrying that I might never find Hereford and the chance for an amusing day, she offered to drive me. My stomach did not encourage too much chat on the two-hour drive from Oxfordshire, across Worcestershire to Hereford, but my chauffeur got me there in good time. Tom Buckingham greeted me with the soon-to-be familiar big smile and I set off to walk the course. To my inexperienced eye there did not appear to be anything too complicated, but I was to learn an awful lot more about the intricacies of riding Hereford in the years ahead. Remarkably I was to be leading jockey there six years on the bounce, but on this occasion I was not aware of what I should take into account, I just wanted to know which way to go and not to make a complete fool of myself. When I got back to the changing room Tom had put my colours up on my peg and told me to get ready. I had not got a saddle of my own and used one of his with the soon-to-be familiar Rimell pad underneath.

I weighed out and my saddle was taken by a lad who had 'been there, done that and got the T-shirt' more times than any champion jockey, Clifford Rawlings, and my stomach took another twist for the worse. I left Tom with a pat on the back and, 'Go on Sam, you can do it,' and went with ten others to the parade ring. Mercy was there waiting for me as Mr Rimell had told me, and I could not miss her as she would have won any 'best turned-out prize', but my God she was formidable and that was even before I had met her! I introduced myself and having spotted my mount All Spirit, number seven, walking around I remarked, 'He looks well,' in as relaxed a tone as I could muster. However, before I could compose myself for something sensible to say, I was taken aback by the large blinkers my precious mount had around his eyes. My stomach took over again and I spluttered, 'I see he wears blinkers, does he not like being hit?' That was the first of many remarks I was to regret uttering to the Queen of NH racing. 'You will not need to hit him,' she responded without a flicker of amusement.

Riding for fun had gone out of the window, and I knew I really did have to deliver. They did both win and Mercy was quite correct, I did not have to use my whip on All Spirit or Seaward Bound; the first won in a canter, the second not so easily, but it won. Being driven home to Banbury I was happy again. I was pleased to ring Mr Rimell up and he was pleased to hear from me. 'Well done lad, I will find another for you before the end of the season.' Theresa and I partied that night and Anthony had had a winner as well so the lid came off the boiling kettle. Next morning I woke with a smile on my face, and memories of a successful day were enjoyed until the morning's responsibilities took over.

Over the next week or two the phone began to ring a lot more than previously and something had definitely changed. I was going racing a lot more, with no great success, but instead of an Irish schoolboy on holiday I was a young man expected to do more than play at riding racehorses, and I wish I had got the message at that very early stage of my career. My growing number of friends on the Point-to-Point circuit were winding down as their season drew to an end and the NH season was dwindling to its customary two-month break before it all started again on the 1st August. I had made up my mind to stay another year in England. The Guv'nor was keen for me to stay and was promising more opportunities as, with the experience I had now gained, my riding allowance of 7lb should be of value to him.

My life was, however, beginning to change, and the first upward drafts of a powerful tornado were beginning to catch me in their grip. My success and the drips of recognition, fuelled by my own belief that I could do it, were beginning to bond into a dangerous combination. Then only a few days before I set off back to Ireland to chase salmon in a wonderful west coast river, the champion trainer rang again, and this time he asked me to come and be his amateur rider for the following season. What a telephone call that was. I was being dealt all the aces and I knew I had to grab the opportunity with both hands. John Webber shrugged his shoulders and muttered, 'After me getting you over here, he is now taking you to enjoy the benefit,' but of course he encouraged me to leave and to grasp the opportunity with both hands – what a generous man he was.

After four weeks back home in Ireland, split between home on Bellewstown Hill and fishing in the west, I arrived at Kinnersley in the first week of July, a small hamlet of red brick and pretty black and white houses and a pub, nestled between the relatively new M5 motorway and the River Severn, not many miles south of Worcester. Mr Rimell greeted me with a warm smile and with understandable pride showed me round the yard. Mid-afternoon it was quiet and immaculate, red brick boxes with freshly painted black wooden doors making a quadrangle for twenty-six expensive thoroughbreds to look out onto an attractive tree-lined yard surrounded by a cobblestone path. In some awe I followed my new boss into each box and he gave me a brief history of each occupant and the individual plans for the season ahead. This was the stuff of dreams and when we explored further lines of boxes and came across last season's Champion Hurdler, Comedy Of Errors, I knew I had not only landed on my feet but on a springboard to stardom.

Having looked at the best part of sixty horses, on our way back through the main yard I was pleased to hear an Irish accent coming from within a smoke-filled room beside an immaculate feed room. 'Jack, come out here,' bellowed my new boss. Slightly hunched, in clothes only just fit for a jumble sale, with six cats around his feet, Jack Kidd the travelling head lad appeared. As Jack had originally suggested to Fred and Mercy that I should be given the opportunity to ride a winner for the yard on that memorable Bank Holiday afternoon at Hereford, he was understandably pleased to see me and I was very pleased to meet him. Thankfully a firm handshake and a genuine welcome were on offer rather than a cup of tea, as Jack and kitchen hygiene obviously did not go hand in hand. He shared his accommodation with his six cats, and on command Benji, one of his favourites, promptly jumped through his outstretched arms. I was soon to find out that this was Jack's party piece to most visitors to the yard. I was, however, very pleased to have a friend close at hand and in the months and years ahead, Jack not only ensured that all the horses I was given the opportunity to win on arrived at the racetrack both in good time and in good order, but very often he put the saddles on too. Indeed, he might well have put a kind word in for me to get the ride in the first place. A good ally to have in the very competitive world I was moving into.

Without much further ado Fred, who throughout my career I addressed as Guv'nor or Sir when I was at the races, then suggested I follow him down to my new digs, a mile away in the village of Severn Stoke. I have no doubt that sometime during the housing boom of the eighties someone might have made a packet out of this property that was to become my home for the best part of two years: 'ideal location, beautiful views over the River Severn, opportunity for large garden and orchard', however, on that summer evening in the mid-seventies it could only be described as a 'small old cottage needing refurbishment'. My accommodation had never been a priority for me; I just needed a bed, somewhere to cook and somewhere to wash. Wall Cottage just about had all three in the small dark rooms, with some peeling damp wallpaper in places, and one very cold bathroom. I was happy to find one of the three bedrooms upstairs empty with the exception of an old steel bed and a pine wardrobe. So as Fred drove out of the short drive from the back of the property – there only was a back door – with instructions for me to be up at the yard at seven o'clock next day, I was quite content to have landed in this school of excellence. The excellence was at Kinnersley not Wall Cottage, which was to see plenty of action over the next two years, but precious little excellence and certainly no refurbishment.

At the Starting Gate

I ARRIVED UP at the yard to find it already a hive of activity at five minutes to seven. I did not get much of a welcome, not at first anyway – a grunt here, a growl there – it was too early for conversation. The rush to have three, four sometimes five mucked out before ten to eight was something that I was not going to enjoy in the weeks, indeed years ahead. I looked out for a friendly face and headed for the feed room in the hope of getting a steer from Jack Kidd, but instead I found the well-oiled engine of Ron Peachey. Head lad, master feeder, master leg man and comedian thrown in. The soft purr of a man who loved his job and loved his horses guided me to a square of sacking cloth and a pitchfork and pointed me to a stable round the back. He was a man of few words but his expressions often told you more. I was welcome, I had already ridden two winners for the yard and as far as Ron was concerned I'd do and thankfully I got the impression that he would point me in the right direction. I don't suppose I mucked that first one out better than I had mucked out any before but I knew that I was not enamoured with this new idea of the muck sack, something else I had to get used to. Having swung the wet sack on my back and dumped the contents where I saw the others dumping theirs, I got my job done on this occasion with time to spare.

Ron found me some tack, which was all in quite good order, and I found my name at the bottom of a list of twenty-two others on a nice wooden board where both horse names and riders could interchange according to Fred's wishes, and I had two horses against mine. The first one was Seaward Bound, one of the horses I had won on at Hereford three months previously. With the clatter of hooves in the yard I pulled out rather nervously, not sure whether I had got all the pads and saddle cloths I had been given in the right order, although a quick glance elsewhere allowed my pulse to settle a little as I seemed to have everything in place correctly. To lose a pad would cause some amusement amongst the other lads, but to give a horse a sore back on my first morning would be extremely careless.

I followed others out onto the road in front of the yard, and it was as if the curtain had just lifted for Act One of a West End musical; from silence and frantic activity there was now a burst of chat and gossip. As we circled in front of the main yard I was soon introduced to everybody, and I was very relieved that I already had those winners in the bag. Taffy, the Welshman who always looked like he had just come off a North Sea oil rig – long hair, half shaven and invariably in heavy yellow oilskins – did most of the introductions as he was at Hereford when I had 'done the business'. Clifford was there that day too; he rode short but looked good on a horse, and could have ridden on the Flat. The two Heath brothers, Mervyn and

Trevor, were as different as chalk and cheese. Mervyn looked after Comedy – he would have slept with him if he could and probably did on some occasions when they went racing overnight, and his world centred around the champion's wellbeing. Trevor was hungry for rides and he saw me as somewhat of an unwelcome rival to his path to an increased wage packet and rides himself.

Jim was on Zarib, another star of the yard, who had won the Triumph Hurdle. Jim was broad and strong but too big to be a jockey although he had a nice happy-go-lucky attitude; I should get on all right with him I thought. Then there was Kevin, a small nail of a man, older than the rest but with a big cheery smile, who had seen many more than me come and go, but if I lessened his work-load around the yard he would be happy. Steve and Michael were two of my companions with whom I shared Wall Cottage. Michael had come straight from school in Wolverhampton, and the way he sat on his horse that morning I could tell he had not seen that many horses – the Aston Villa football team was his passion.

Then there were of course the jockeys. Ken White, the number one, was not in that morning but John Burke was and he was friendly enough in his quiet Irish way, as was the yard's conditional jockey Richard O'Donovan. They were well aware that new competition for those precious rides had been thrown into the mix. Luckily I was never going to find well-deserved congratulations difficult and I knew we were likely to share a lot of ups and downs but there was also fierce competition. Not unlike single lions in the bush, we were competing for similar reward and with only a limited amount at our disposal a missed chance could mean an opportunity missed for personal gain in the future. Not the best circumstances for close friendships.

The full team of twenty-two were soon out – a very mixed bunch of twenty lads, with two girls adding colour and a target for ridicule and fun – and then Mercy appeared on her rather angular grey hack, Bucket. A certain hush enveloped us like a cloud, reins were gathered up, chatting groups of twos and threes moved into line and without a word the long string took on an orderly shape in military fashion. I soon found myself shuffled to the back of the string next to the remarkably immaculate Mercy. Over the years I was to learn that Mercy was always immaculate, whether in the kitchen, the drawing room or even the bedroom. We were summoned there one day – another scary experience – but she was always fit for a 'best turned-out' prize, and this first morning was no exception. She could not have been more welcoming and with an instruction from Fred, now standing with his arms folded outside the yard in front of his house, we set off through the small hamlet of Kinnersley for Deer Park less than a mile away, for two gentle canters. This was the start of a routine I was going to enjoy, with only a few exceptions, for a number of years.

I was quickly enough into the routine. It was an efficient set-up – smart horses needed a smart operation – and I was impressed by it all and went home in the evenings full of expectations. My housemates and I had found the pub, The Royal Oak, just across the road from

Wall Cottage in the village of Severn Stoke but we had found little else and our evenings were quiet. Peace did not last long as only halfway through that first week I heard a rumour that a friend of the Webbers, Kim Bailey, whom I had met briefly at Stratford during the summer when he was assistant trainer to Captain Tim Forster, was joining Fred as his assistant.

Riding out, Mercy confirmed that the rumour was true and we were to make room for him in Wall Cottage. A screech of tyres signalled his arrival that evening. A British racing green MGB GT Sports Coupé jolted to a stop within feet of our small front door. Lying almost horizontal – I was to find out over the months and years ahead that he regularly took up this position and it was not always in the car or the bedroom – was Bailey. Big smile, firm confident handshake. Provided I could hold my own I could see that we would get on well and our spare time was certainly not going to be dull in future. 'What a dump,' he exclaimed, 'let's go to the pub for supper.'

The Royal Oak in Severn Stoke gradually became our home. None of us drank much, it was a miracle we were not thrown out for too much noise and not drinking enough at times. However, even in those early days, crisps, nuts and beer in half-pints went a long way to being our evening meal, and we were soon to add a bag of fresh tomatoes to that mixture. Cyril and his brother Derek ran the place as if it was their home and they made us very welcome at all times of the night and day. They never gave the impression of being shrewd businessmen, but racing chat and a tip or two from the local stable did attract the more affluent punters as the weeks went by, and they knew more than we did on how to run a successful public house.

The draughts of my tornado were soon to catch me in their grip again. I was put on the first two runners of the new season, little Seaward Bound at Newton Abbot and Hanzon at Hereford and they both won. Two rides, two winners, I was the blue-eyed boy and hardly knew different. I got beaten on both these two next time out, but momentum was not lost when I was told that one of the best young horses in the yard, a beautiful looking little mare called Mrs Parsons, was going to run at Kempton Park, the first televised race meeting of the season in the first week of October. I was nervous on this bigger stage, big racecourse and a much bigger crowd than I was used to. It was a handicap hurdle for amateur riders, but the little mare was an easy ride and everything fell into place beautifully, as we led on the run-in and won by half a length. A strong upward gust of wind caught me that day.

The next televised meeting was at Chepstow and once again I felt in the limelight. Fred ran three in the Free Handicap Hurdle and I rode the third choice Brief Authority, with Ken and John on the other two. I knew he was a well-thought-of youngster and how privileged I was to be allowed to ride him. He finished midfield, much as Fred and Mercy anticipated, but I remember being pleased as I had beaten one of our other two runners. The following Saturday I was again thrust into the spotlight, on television again with Mrs Parsons in the Tom

Masson Trophy at Newbury. This was one of the early highlights of the season for young potential hurdling stars. Many of the top professionals of the day, including Jeff King, John Francome and others were riding in the race and Mrs Parsons was a warm favourite after her impressive display at Kempton a fortnight earlier. In a very competitive race we had every chance at the last but got beaten by a length. The first taste of disappointment for a while, although there was going to be plenty more in the years ahead, but this particular wave of success was hardly jolted by this single reverse.

I was now beginning to appreciate how this unique and very successful team of Fred and Mercy worked. Fred, with the help of Ron Peachey, prepared the horses for battle and Mercy decided where she thought they would win, and she also had a fair say in who would ride them and fired most of the arrows. Once a week we seemed to have schooling sessions, and I soon got the impression that Fred liked his young horses to stand back and be confident. 'Kick 'em in Sam,' he would shout. I had always been taught to 'kick 'em in', so kick I did and with these small fences it tended to work well and Fred and Mercy liked what they saw. I know now that these instructions were to be very detrimental to my future career, but I was blind to see the error of my ways for far too long and only have myself to blame.

I was somewhat surprised when another good horse was entered in an amateur race the following week; someone still had some faith. Bramblestown was not such an easy ride, although we ran well but got beaten on my first visit to Ludlow, which was going to become another happy hunting ground. However, I was allowed back on the lovely mare Mrs Parsons only a fortnight later at Cheltenham, my first ride at the Mecca of NH racing. Fred's good mare had frightened all the other runners away and only one stood their ground to take us on but Mrs Parsons was such a long odds-on shot that no betting was recorded. No betting meant nothing to me at the time while the supposed certainty of the result did, but fortunately she carried me impeccably to the line and we won by a distance at 10/1 on. I doubt a Cheltenham winner has ever been as easy and I was the lucky one to be on top.

I was now beginning to get some outside rides, and Doug Marks asked me to travel right across the south of England to Fontwell where, unbeknown to me, he landed a nice little touch on Revise in an amateur handicap hurdle. Doug Marks always seemed to be smiling, but apparently he was laughing all the way to the bank that day. Hugh O'Neill also had me travelling across the country to racecourses that I had not been to before.

The familiar faces to welcome me were always either John or Tom Buckingham, my valets, and when there was only one meeting in the south they were both there. They arrived at each meeting sometimes as early as 9am. They got all their jockeys' gear out, cleaned all the boots and a huge collection of saddles from tiny 2lb ones to the majority which were between 5lb and 8lb. Along with these they needed a large number of weight cloths and saddle pads. All this had to be shipshape and Bristol fashion before the thirty or so jockeys riding that day appeared, normally about two hours before the first race.

The season was now getting into full swing and there was a buzz of excitement in the yard. Life in Wall Cottage was fine – a bed and food, of questionable quality, cooked by ourselves, sufficed us well. Bailey quite often appeared with a bit of talent on his arm, although Wall Cottage was not quite the accommodation he would have preferred. My good mate Tocky came to see us occasionally, but perhaps to her annoyance I was too wrapped up in my horses at the time and certainly did not give her the attention she deserved.

I was now away once or twice a week so I was lucky to avoid a lot of the monotony of stable work. I mucked out my three in the morning, rode three lots and if I was not racing did my three up in the evening. None of my three were due to run for some time, as I was not good enough at this part of the job to be allowed anything any good. The senior lads had first choice of all the good ones and my chances of even having a runner were very slim. A full day in the yard was a long day and I was always very glad when Ron would signal that it was time to feed. I did learn some new skills and to try and impress Fred on his evening walk around the stables, putting a neat twist in the straw at the entrance of your stable gave a much needed indication of care and dedication. This did not fool Fred for long as one occasion, having done this with great care, dampened my charge's mane and tail and had everything looking what I thought was immaculate, he found me fast asleep in the corner of my stable. I have always been a morning person.

The stable buzz reached a crescendo with Comedy having his first run of the season at Newcastle and we had Royal Frolic, a potential champion, running at Wolverhampton. On arriving into the yard that morning I soon got the message that John was injured and the boys thought I would be riding this young star at Wolverhampton. Fred was soon out and about and confirmed this exciting news. I already had two other rides on the day but they paled into insignificance with this news. The other two got beaten but, much to my relief, Frolic won. He was by far the most exciting ride over fences I had ever had, because he had the most wonderful agility and was so powerful; he was going to become a good friend.

Christmas came with the expectations of the big Kempton meeting and the King George. Comedy would run somewhere, probably the New Year's Day Hurdle at Windsor, and we would have a host of runners at Wolverhampton. Kim came up trumps as, thanks to a ride and a winner for me on Skybound for his father earlier in the month, I had met Colonel and Jill Sidgwick, Skybound's owners, and they very kindly invited me for lunch on Christmas Day. It was a great invitation to receive and I was saved crisps and nuts in the Royal Oak and instead greatly enjoyed like-minded souls in a lovely country house in the hills overlooking Cheltenham.

I was home in good time as Fred had me jocked up for three at Wolverhampton. Brown Admiral, whom I was going to ride in the Grand National the following year, won the big race of the day and I was second on another one so I was content on the short drive back to Wall Cottage that night. No joy for the yard at Kempton and Comedy got beaten at Windsor on New Year's Day – beware of Mercy when things were not going to plan! I had by now learnt that being last in the string meant being first in line for the fearsome wrath of the First Lady. Mind you, Kim and I still enjoyed our breakfast where Fred's humour, despite almost any disaster the day before, could bring little else but a smile to your face.

I was now getting quite a lot more rides for outside stables and some of these were winning. None for the big yards, as in those days they all had one, if not two, of their own jockeys, but smaller stables who wanted to make the most of my inexperienced rider's allowance which was diminishing fast. I drove myself down to Taunton to ride in the hunter chase for a small trainer I had never met, but his small convenience buried me at the third fence, and much to my indignation I woke up in hospital. With nothing more than a severe headache I promptly discharged myself, informing those caring for me that I had to get home and there was nothing wrong with me. A very foolhardy approach that I was going to regret as my head continued to get battered on an all too regular basis in the years ahead. I can't remember now how I ever got home; the immediate time span around this bashing of my cranium is a complete blank, as it was going to be many times in the future. I would have benefited from someone explaining the dangers of concussion at this early stage of my career, but whether I would have listened remains to be seen.

A week later I was riding again and Fred's horses were running well. John Burke then showed us all why he was such a good jockey when coaxing the very broad Rag Trade to a clear round and a memorable win in the Welsh National, which in 1976 was run in the third week of January. Soon afterwards John got injured and Fred gave me the leg up on Royal Frolic again, this time in the Greenall Whitley at Haydock in the third week of February. This was my biggest race to date, BBC cameras and a big prize. I went predominantly round the outside of this big galloping track giving my extravagant jumper plenty of room to jump. Frolic jumped from fence to fence and he won with something in hand, with Red Rum and others trailing in his wake. The following morning whispers of Frolic's future plans were on everyone's lips, and the local bookmaker in Upton-upon-Severn took far more money that he should have for Royal Frolic to win the Cheltenham Gold Cup in a month's time.

The run up to Cheltenham was like nothing I had witnessed before. We had Comedy to defend his Champion Hurdle crown, Frolic in the Gold Cup and four or five other runners, Brown Admiral being one of them in one of the other big races. Every step, every move was taken with care; it was as if all the horses were being asked to walk on glass. The clockwork timing of the yard became precision timing, the feeding became even more complex than it was previously, Ron took on a focus that had previously been hidden behind the face of humour and generosity we were used to, Jack Kidd had less time for his cats and polished tack religiously all day, while Fred studied more legs than a judge at a Miss World contest. The Cheltenham Festival was an unknown theatre to me but the build-up was not going to lead to an anti-climax.

A First Taste of the Big Time

KITTED OUT IN my best suit, I arrived in plenty of time. Already three hours before the first, the crowds were huge, the buzz electric. I was to ride a little mare called Quickapenny in the third race of the meeting, the Joe Coral Hurdle Final, for Mrs Courage. The jockeys' changing room had a huge air of expectation about it. Gone were the jokes and daily pranks played by the regular jesters and the mass of top Irish jockeys over for the meeting provided added colour to that inner sanctum. All my heroes from home were over and I was set to ride against them in this great battle for supremacy. The meeting could not have started much better for me. Quickapenny travelled well, and, fazed by the big occasion less than her jockey, she led two out to be run out of it up the notorious Cheltenham hill to finish second. She had run well above expectations and a big local following showed me for the first time what it would be like to ride a winner during these three hallowed days.

The draughts of my tornado caught my shirt-tails and the rest of the meeting went with a swirl. Comedy got beaten by Night Nurse in the Champion Hurdle, I had a great ride on my old favourite Brown Admiral in the Mildmay, leading again two out to finish fourth, and on Thursday, the final day of the meeting, Royal Frolic ridden by a now fully-recovered John Burke won the Gold Cup. Bula was the warm fancy at 6/4, and our star started at 14/1, but he jumped his rivals into the ground, led at the third last and won by five lengths from Brown Lad and Tommy Carberry. The small bookmaker in Upton-upon-Severn was the only unhappy local that evening. Fred and Mercy, Ron and Kim and nearly all the rest of the team had taken the 250/1 that was offered immediately after Frolic had won at Haydock a month earlier, crucially before it was announced that he was going to run in the Gold Cup.

I was not a betting man – losing a tenner hurt me more than the joy of winning forty – so I was left out of this particular bonanza, more fool me on this occasion. However, serious success with my first big bet could have lit a fuse which would have been hard to put out. Thankfully, apart from the Gay Future disaster, I was never ever tempted. The winning bets of others paled into insignificance when measured against the skill of training and placing this lively youngster to beat all the odds and become a champion. We all left Cheltenham in a haze, the Royal Oak threw us out late and back in the yard at seven the next day we only went through the motions, but that did not matter – we had won the Gold Cup! The Upton-upon-Severn bookmaker went out of business.

The horses were back in form, John was soon back in the winner's enclosure and I rode our fast little grey, a bit of a runaway, Zip Fastener to win easily at Doncaster. In a matter of no time Aintree and the Grand

National were looming. Ten days before the meeting I got one of the more magical telephone calls in that early stage of my career when Frank Cundell rang to ask me to ride Ballybright in the big race. I was over the moon and soon got swept up by the magical build-up to this great race. Having won the Welsh National with Rag Trade the yard had every reason to be excited about his chances in the big one, but all I could think about was my first ride over the big fences. Not that I did much about it, I just waited and prayed that nothing would go wrong before the big day.

With no rides on the first two days of the three-day meeting I drove up on Saturday morning listening to Sport on Four coming from Aintree, with a rich flow of adrenalin pouring through my system. The atmosphere at Aintree was different to the tense drama of Cheltenham and the jockeys' changing room reflected a relaxed happy atmosphere. In the race before the Grand National, Comedy made up for his defeat at Cheltenham by winning the big hurdle race, and I congratulated Fred as he took John's saddle for Rag Trade in high spirits. I met Mr Cundell for the first time and gave him my new lightweight saddle bought with this or similar occasions in mind. Ballybright was set to carry the minimum weight of 10st and I wanted the most comfortable saddle I could find for this marathon.

The changing room was full of chat of who's going where – it was the outside for me. 'I don't trust your yoke', 'if you're going there I'm going down the middle', 'you will never get round on that thing', 'sod you boys

I'm up the inside, follow me if you dare'. Witnessing this for the first time was mind-blowing and it was always going to be the same in the future. I had made no plans, because as far as I was concerned if luck was with me I would win, if not, too bad it was great to have the chance. Hardly the right attitude of a semi-professional sportsman but with all this talk about luck, foolishly I never thought much further than that element of luck in this high octane contest.

Once loosed from the claustrophobic clutches of the huge crowd and long parade, the freedom galloping down to look at the first fence was breathtaking. I had walked around that morning and had my first look at the awesome fences, and on little Ballybright they looked no smaller, but a row of crashed cars would not have stopped me now.

The tapes went up and the roar of the crowd sent us off like the cavalry in the Battle of Corunna. Despite being asked by an ageing steward not to go too quickly down to the first, we seemed to be going very very fast, and the first wall of green firs came at us like an Atlantic wave on my favourite Donegal beach – the crash of fir, the thud of hooves, the expletives from excited jockeys. One fell all too close to me; another was down in the middle but I was clear and on to the next. No trouble there, little Ballybright seemed to be enjoying it but it was the huge ditch next, and somehow we were over that. Two more and then a steady roar went up as the jockeys in front exclaimed to each other that Becher's was next, and like a swarm of bees swaying in the wind we all found ourselves swinging slightly to the right to get a slight angle over the big drop; there was some grief but we were still in the hunt. The tightness of the Canal Turn caught me by surprise but once straightened up for the first time I had a look around to see who else was still at the races.

I saw John and Rag Trade going well but he was too far ahead of me to speak to. Big Ron Barry, who was never short of a word during a race, and The Dikler, were upsides and dwarfing Red Rum and Tommy Stack. They seemed to be having some animated conversation about something, but I was not going to say anything to the grown-ups and I contented myself to listening to the other chat going on around me. 'I nearly went at Becher's but he's jumping well now,' and 'we're knackered, I think I will pull up before the Chair,' whilst a few more expletives came echoing towards me between the thunder of hooves.

I still had some horse under me and I would at least beat you, I thought, looking at a tired horse's head by my right boot. We jumped the enormous Chair and headed back out into the country again, but Ballybright was tiring a little and so was I. We met Becher's all wrong, stumbled on landing and the Aintree turf hit me in the face for the first time. My National was all over, no disappointment, just complete elation that I had taken part. A lift in a patrol car got me back in time to watch John and Rag Trade complete a fantastic season for Fred, winning him his fourth Grand National, in the same season he had won his second Gold Cup, Woodland Venture with Terry Biddlecombe on top being his other some nine years earlier.

To round the day off nicely I had a spin round in the amateur hurdle, historically the race after the big one. The ride did not amount to anything and I don't remember much about it, but I hoped one day I would enjoy success in front of this huge animated crowd. A final twist to the day came when John Buckingham and I could not find my new lightweight saddle. I went out to the Trainers' Bar to find Mr Cundell, while making a point of thanking him for giving me the ride and asking how Ballybright was, before enquiring whether he still had my saddle. Without undue concern he told me that he had given it to a helpful young fellow who said he was going to be going past the weighing room and would drop it in. The young fellow might have been going that way but he never dropped it in. My trusting trainer had been duped by some lowlife and I never saw my smart lightweight saddle again. In the giddy heights of that evening the loss hardly registered, as I was still galloping towards Becher's in seventh heaven.

I was now firmly in the grip of my personal tornado, flying high with more cash in my pocket than I had ever had before and I had done little more than sat on a few good horses and kept kicking. Just before Cheltenham I had been told that I was seven clear in the Amateur Championship. Fred was aware of this and he was keen to try and help me maintain this lead until the end of the season in the first week of June. However, the very dry spring of 1976 meant that he and Mercy had taken the wise decision to turn out to grass the vast majority of their string. His big arm went around my shoulder and he told me that he was sorry he could not do much to help me, but he would keep a couple of horses on the go that liked fast ground and he would put me up on those when possible. He gave me the leg up on Donnybrook twice during May – we won on both occasions – and I scrambled a few outside rides but found no other winners.

The season ended with two fun days at Stratford; everyone was in holiday mood and it was time to get off the treadmill. One of my local rivals, George Jones, had a late flurry of winners and Peter Greenall, now Lord Daresbury, had his northern firepower in fine form and just beat me to a previously impossible dream of being Amateur Champion. It could have meant a lot more to me at the time, and perhaps should have done, but I had far exceeded my own expectations. Fred had invited me back next season and wanted me to turn professional. It seemed a natural progression and like many other things I did not give it much thought. I was about to step into a career as a professional jockey, too confident of my own ability with only one string to my bow.

Life in the Fast Lane

THAT SUMMER MY feet hardly touched the ground. Bailey, Oliver Sherwood and I spent ten days on a square-rigged cutter in the Mediterranean, living a life way beyond my previous expectations. I had my first water ski and of course crashed into the boat. We laughed for ten days – if this was the result of riding racehorses for a living I could manage more of it! Back to Ireland to see Mum and Dad briefly before the west coast salmon rivers and hopefully a day or two on Lough Mask beckoned again and I was off on another adrenalin rush.

Lough Mask is one of the unique jewels of Ireland. Lying in a limestone basin in the south eastern corner of Mayo, it provides wonderful feeding for beautiful big spotted brown trout in clear, often relatively shallow, water. I have had the joy of fishing this lovely lough with the help and guidance of one of the Mask's most respected boatman, John Maye, a lovely softly spoken Mayo man. He is still taking clients out, although now an octogenarian, and I have been fortunate to enjoy many happy days with him, after many years of trying I was very fortunate to catch a specimen trout a few years ago.

The river I was heading for after the joys of this lovely lough is the Owenmore River which is another jewel of

Connaught. Its catchment is a wide area from the northern slopes of Nephin Beg across the low plain of western Mayo parallel to the southern cliffs of Donegal Bay back west almost to Belmullet. Sloping bog surrounded by gentle windswept granite slopes provides the sparkling golden flow that tempts thousands of salmon to return to their spawning grounds year after year. Rich pickings were caught in the many miles of drift nets off the coast, but just enough salmon run the gauntlet successfully to reach their birthplace as strong silver arrows ready to ensure their precious life cycle is started once again. Casting a fly over their resting places, often only hinted at by the indication from a change in current caused by a hidden boulder, is the stuff of happy dreams. The rod dips, a little patience to let him turn, then hopefully feeling him, lifting your rod and the excitement begins. Escapism at its best, although I needed to catch a lot of salmon to calm me down after the year that had seen me reach for the stars; but I am sure we caught a few.

I got back to Kinnersley at the beginning of the second week of July which coincided with most of the horses were coming back in from their own summer holidays. Fred was his usual cheerful self and told me to hurry up and get my professional licence sorted. Ken White had retired so John Burke was now set as stable jockey and Richard O'Donovan and I would be sharing second pickings. I did not really take in the importance of my role; getting paid for doing something I loved was as far as it registered. Before the season got underway in a fortnight's time there was too much grooming for my liking and hours of roadwork on very unfit horses to put up with. Thankfully I was one of the lucky ones riding a canter first lot most mornings, on the small string of horses who were being aimed at some of the early races on the West Country circuit at the beginning of the season.

After breakfast with Fred and Mercy, which Kim and I thoroughly enjoyed, we set off for two long jogs around the local lanes. On most of our routes we made sure we took the way past one of the many orchards in the area so we could at least fill our pockets with a wide range of Worcestershire apples. Wall Cottage had changed little, dust was everywhere and there was growth in the fridge that was worthy of a sixth form case study; the Royal Oak was a more attractive proposition for a few days. An urgent clean-up was required when we received news that a new lodger was arriving shortly to share our den.

Nigel Twiston-Davies made a less than flamboyant entry into our lives in a cream Morris Marina littered with old and nearly new clothes, boots and shoes all over the place and we had to wonder why we had bothered to clean up the house. The pub was the only option that evening, and a few drinks later I knew that a pretty potent mix had been added to our small social circle. Things got even better when Fred announced that he had invested in a building plot in Ryall, a small hamlet just outside Upton-upon-Severn, and only two miles from the yard. For the time being Nigel piled his belongings into the vacant bedroom in Wall Cottage, and we were also joined by Kim's dog, Boozer. He could only have found him in a dogs' home, a pitch black curly mop, bred in a back-street alley with a cheeky smile on his face and obedience to match.

A list of the local talent was soon drawn up: the new bird at the Esso station up the road was worth a visit, and the twins up at Castlemorton and their horsey mate appeared game for anything. Then of course there was the smart Gloucestershire set whose attentions required a more serious strategic plan to tempt them in this direction, although Kim and Nigel had their noses much more on the scent than I did. I was not used to being out-performed, but their tireless approach to achieving another notch on the headboard caused endless amusement.

Boozer played his part in being a cuddly point of conversation for the latest conquest, to obediently awaiting his master's return from his afternoon in the bedroom and showing great appreciation for everyone's happiness. On one wonderful occasion he slipped into the bedroom where Bailey had bedded his latest conquest, snatched the pair of discarded pink knickers from the floor and was next seen throwing these in the air while playing in the mud outside our back door. Nigel and I enjoyed watching Bailey smooth this mishap over, but poor Boozer never realised why his boss was so distraught.

The drought which had brought the season to a premature end at Kinnersley was still with us through this late summer and autumn. The ground was firm nearly everywhere and Fred and Mercy were not keen to run anything, and worse still they had no intention of getting the horses fit until we had some rain. There were small fields when the season opened at Newton Abbot in the first week of August, and Devon and Exeter on top of Haldon Hill was like the proverbial road. The first two Hereford meetings were abandoned, as was Huntingdon and Sedgefield in the north. I had my first ride as a professional on Donnybrook at Bangor on the 24th August 1976. We made all and held on to win by a length, hard ridden. Fred was chuffed and within a couple of days presented me with a tankard suitably engraved, which I have to this day. Unfortunately, adulation was the last thing I needed.

Nothing much had changed, as getting paid to ride was of little value since the rides available were few and far between. Now that I had lost my claim the small trainers that had used me before saw little value in my services now and Fred would not let his main string of horses hit the racecourse. My old friends Seaward Bound and Hanzon were now being ridden by Nigel, who had taken my place as the amateur in the yard. Being the new boy in the team, the entertaining first lot shuffle ensured that he was regularly manoeuvred back to last place, one in front of Mercy each morning, besides which we knew he had work to do to keep the rides.

Late night parties in our new house in Ryall were becoming all too regular and Nigel was a party animal. One memorable morning when we knew he needed to be on his best behaviour, as he was due to ride Seaward Bound at the weekend, he was feeling particularly ill. Much to our amusement we knew he was only just coping to hide the effects of an alcohol overdose when within two minutes of home and safety, he felt the contents of his stomach cry out for a quick discharge. Thankfully he was already dismounted at this stage and, while carrying on a polite conversation with Mercy five yards behind him, he took off his yellow crash helmet, which we all had to wear, and allowed the contents of his stomach to empty into it while managing to carry on the conversation with the Queen of NH racing, without her knowing any better. He kept the ride on Seaward Bound that week.

My own social life had now taken a serious turn for the better; Nigel had introduced me to his sister Penelope, and it was love at first sight. I was besotted, she was a darling, all bounce and go, gorgeous blonde hair and game for anything. I was still on a major high from my amateur season with Fred and this was the icing on the cake. We were ready to party and party we did. We blasted rock 'n' roll from my new sports car lookalike to the West End and, wrapped deep in the euphoria of love, crashed the new car into an old Bentley in Knightsbridge before being swept away by the wonders of the Rocky Horror Show. I had found a kindred spirit and the highs of riding winners had been replaced by the excitement of love.

It had almost passed me by that the first two Cheltenham fixtures were off due to the drought and instead of a host of runners at the first Chepstow meeting we only had one, which John rode. I did have two spins up at Bangor, but both finished down the field. Finally, well into October and probably only half-fit myself, I was put in the hot seat in a televised Wills Premier Chase Qualifier at Newbury on the small but speedy Zip Fastener. We were third favourite and in front turning into the straight for the last time when we took a heavy fall, and I landed awkwardly on my wrist. It was sore and the racecourse doctor was obliged to put a dreaded entry in my medical book to ensure that I could not ride again until I had been passed by another doctor, so it was a long drive home in the back of the Jaguar with Fred and Mercy.

I learnt nothing from this fall and took it as no more than bad luck, believing I had met the fence on an awkward stride and down we went. If I had had half a brain at the time and was taking my career seriously I would have played the video continually (if it had been available) until I had seen what I had done wrong. Today's jockeys would have almost certainly sought tuition from Yogi Breisner, an expert horseman and world-renowned tutor, but no, I was brave and thought that I could ride with the best of them, and I put it down, as with the rest of my falls, to no more than bad luck. To me the point was proved on my second ride back three weeks later when Zip Fastener and I trotted up in a bad race at Bangor. Thanks, not for the first time, were due to Mercy for a clever bit of placing, as it was a bad race and Zip Fastener was streets better than his opponents.

We were well into November and although the ground had now changed we had precious few runners and I had even less rides. Zip Fastener kept my flame burning by enjoying the fast Ludlow circuit and winning another slightly more competitive novice chase, but the yard was in the doldrums. I was not too concerned as life at Plot 9, our House in Ryall, had become the greatest of fun; Kim,

Nigel and I had become good friends and we partied a lot. I took Penelope out as often as I could, away from the inquisitive eyes of her brother and Bailey and put up with the ribbing when I got home. Nigel and Penelope lived deep into Herefordshire and, with Bailey's home being near Brackley, our party range had now become very extensive and very few opportunities to dine out were turned down, so cooking was not something we did very often in Plot 9.

Riding out each morning contained far more tales of the night before and not enough concentrating on the important jobs we were meant to be doing. I don't suppose this went unnoticed by Fred and Mercy, although Fred was always keen to hear the chat over breakfast. Now that the ground had changed, a long string of horses went down to the Park schooling grounds at least once a week. We had to ride over a fairly narrow bridge over the new M5 Motorway, which on a young horse was always exciting, and then turn into a lovely old park with a horseshoe shaped mile and a quarter gallop and three small fences. We would all canter round and then Fred would instruct John, Richard and I to get onto various horses according to his wishes. Mercy would invariably walk up to near the fences to watch the action closely. It was about the only time that I got an indication of how Fred and Mercy thought I was riding and it was always a nervous moment seeing which horse you were going to be asked to school as that invariably meant you were likely to be going to ride that in its next race. Once on board I enjoyed the schooling. The fences were small, the horses fresh and I could get away with my technique of seeing a stride and kicking them in for a spectacular jump, which I knew was exactly what Fred wanted to see.

The big Hennessy meeting at Newbury loomed up. John was to ride Rag Trade and I found myself on Andy Pandy in the big race itself, my first ride in the Hennessy. I had one school on Andy Pandy before, and it was going to be the only time I rode him in a race. We started slowly, made some late headway but never got in the hunt. He only had 10st 9lb and on some of his later form should have finished much closer, but as Rag Trade also ran poorly, in the end falling at the second last, perhaps the horses were a bit off colour. December remained quiet, although I did manage to sprain my wrist again when falling on one of my few mounts that month; I must learn not to put my hand out.

But time and Ron's expertise provided an explosion of form from the yard immediately after Christmas. I won the first two races of the day at Wolverhampton on Double Negative and Brown Admiral, John won the fourth on Hill Top and the following day John won on Royal Gaye and I won on Zip Fastener. Kinnersley was buzzing again. The run continued through January and February – I had plenty of rides while John kept notching up the winners. He got the best out of Andy Pandy and won a National Trial on him and I assumed that my reputation was intact after winning on Double Negative, not the easiest of rides, at the big Schweppes meeting at Newbury.

I was, however, on a slippery slope, riding too tight up the inside at Hereford on a young novice of Fred's having his first run, and he darted out through the wing. We were both OK thank goodness, but Mercy lay the blame firmly on me. We had very few runners at Cheltenham that year, and my old servant Brown Admiral was my only ride although I wrestled him to the ground in the Grand Annual. I was beginning to feel the pressure, as everything I rode was pushed and kicked to the limit with not always the best results. John Burke, my competitor for rides in the yard, was in my view at the time far too relaxed and quiet on the stable's runners. Mercy liked his style and once again I should have taken note of the many things that he was doing well and not crashed on regardless with the mistaken view that I was the better rider. Needless to say the chaotic life at Plot 9 carried on apace. Bailey was sniffing out some serious Gloucester talent, while Nigel was always chasing talent closer to home, although much to his annoyance he was regularly interrupted by Bailey arriving back early having failed in his quest further afield.

Aintree was soon upon us, and we had Andy Pandy and Brown Admiral in the National, with Andy Pandy looking like starting favourite, and needless to say I was excited about my chances on Brown Admiral. The magic of Aintree swept me along once again; I rode little Zip Fastener in the first race on the Saturday of the big day and he ran well enough and then I got ready for the National. Andy Pandy was all the rage while nearly all the jockeys had some reason to fancy theirs. The excitement was fever pitch and the build-up magical once again, but this time I knew my mount well and looked forward to the challenge. John said he was going handy down the middle and I reckoned I would not be far away from him – that was the plan anyway. The wonderful buzz had certainly hit me again, and as we walked in line out to the parade ring to get mounted, we passed the Owners' and Trainers' Bar, where there was a nice glass of champagne sitting on the window ledge. I thought this would just do me good, grabbed it and knocked it back. To my horror it was a very old gin and tonic, and the horrible taste stuck with me throughout the whole excitement that was to follow. Silly move. The Admiral jumped carefully and well as we got over Becher's and had a good run around to the Chair which we jumped in about fifth place. I saw John and Andy Pandy going well just in front of us and, as we stretched down to Becher's again, he started to pull clear of us all. It was there that once again my dream came to a crashing end, as the Admiral was caught out by the big drop. I was foolishly going the brave man's route down the inside where the drop was the biggest, and he could not stay on his legs. There on the Aintree turf beside me was John who had been going so well and was in fact well clear at the time. We travelled back in the same car to see Red Rum and Ginger McCain in the winner's enclosure for the third time, this time with Tommy Stack on board.

I had a couple more winners before the season drew to a close, but I was beginning to realise that the profession I had sailed into on a wave of success was not going to be a walk in the park. Competition to get rides in the first place was fierce and I had by no means taken all the winning opportunities I was given. I had not changed my style of riding since Fred appeared to be on my side when things went wrong, as indeed they had done on quite a number of occasions. After my last ride of the season in the first week of June, I drove back to Ireland with a fishing rod rather than a whip in my hand.

Discarded on the Muck Heap

I ARRIVED BACK at Kinnersley looking forward to the new season, with plenty of good horses to ride. I felt I had established myself as the number two in the yard and hoped to be sharing most of the rides once the season got going. Fred and Mercy were hugely respected and were known to have one of the best strings in the country, and I was in an enviable position and relished the task ahead. As usual in mid-July most of the string were only just coming in from grass and it appeared we had hardly anything for an early-season campaign. I knew that the real rewards for a jump jockey came when the big meetings started in October so if that was Fred's plan, so be it. Besides Kim, Nigel and I had plenty of other things to think about.

Village cricket was a must and we were doing our best to get a competent team from the yard practised and ready for a match each Sunday. The pub still provided an hour or two of entertainment over lunch and then of course there was the local, or not so local, talent to look after. I was still mad on Penelope and I was not going to let her far from my sight and the fear of any indiscretion being reported back by her brother made sure that I was happy to watch any developments made by my two housemates rather than take part. Discussion most days centred around which bit of talent should be targeted and whether to go for a comparatively easy catch close at hand or put reputations at risk with the Gloucestershire party set.

It was all very entertaining, although one morning I was far from happy, as I had had another fall, and with slight concussion had decided that the best thing for me to do was stay in bed for the morning and not ride out. I was not feeling great and thought a bit of TLC from a good-looking bird in a neighbouring house would be very welcome. I made contact and told her that Bailey and Nigel would be away soon after seven so a visit any time after that would be great, and she said she would be able to come and see me soon after ten. With my two mates well gone, I lay back thinking how far I would get when the sexy neighbour came and sat on my bed, and what form her tender loving care would take. My imagination was running riot when the door into Plot 9 opened, and much to my consternation it was Bailey. 'Just back for a quick cup of tea,' he murmured. I knew his timing could seriously mess up my plans and I prayed he would take his tea with him and go. Alas, I then heard voices; my likely masseuse had arrived. I waited patiently for Bailey to do the honourable thing and leave us alone, never thinking he would do anything else. I waited and waited but all had gone quiet. Eventually in desperation I climbed from my sick bed only to find both Bailey and my likely masseuse half naked on the kitchen floor. So much for your friends, and my headache took a turn for the worse!

As our horses got fit I should have been getting fit myself but I never thought a visit to the gym or cycling without a saddle was necessary, and with a few races under my belt I reckoned that I would soon be fit enough. Dieting was not necessary either, as our habit of a bag of tomatoes and a half-pint in the pub was the odd mixture and routine we had got into. The thought of trying to eat a balanced diet was unheard of and not something we ever talked about either at home or with my growing band of mates in the changing room at the races. Sadly, it never occurred to me that the reason why I was often very tired at the end of a day's racing was because I was eating all the wrong types of food, and this was going to be a problem right through my career. Advice at this early stage would have been very helpful, but of course I did not go looking for it.

As the season got going my relaxed mood began to change into one of some anxiety and impatience. While we had no horses ready to run, many of the other yards were beginning to churn out winners and more importantly some of my contemporaries were riding them. Graham McCourt was having a great start to the season and I reckoned I was far more experienced than he was at the time; George Jones, my ex-amateur rival had been in the winner's enclosure as well. As August went by I got more and more restless and frustrated, although I had lots to look forward to. I was not enjoying sitting at home and having to check the morning papers each day to see which of my mates had been successful. It was 1976 and that year was to be remembered for being one of the hottest summers for many years, with hosepipe restrictions in many parts of the country. It was a nightmare for those racecourses that had not got their own water supply and the resulting very fast ground had come at the wrong time for me.

Unknown to me Kim was getting restless as well. He had spent two seasons with Captain Tim Foster in Lambourn and had now two seasons with Fred and Mercy. He certainly had the credentials to start training on his own and he felt the time was right for him to give it a go. His father Ken had not been well, and he was not enjoying training his small string anymore. With his wife Biddy they were a great pair, both lovers of the countryside and all things sporting. It was not long before Kim had runners in his own right and history relates huge success. Despite playing hard he had obviously learnt a lot. I was not learning enough myself and sadly the Plot 9 party had started to disintegrate.

I had my first ride of the new season three weeks into August on a lovely mare called Apple Of My Eye trained by Fred. She was well named and ran a blinder to finish second. Unfortunately, next morning she was lame and out for the season. This was a blow as Fred always left a little to work on so she would have improved from her first run and if I had kept the ride we could have won two or three. More horses began to come on stream through September into October but still precious little was happening, although there were more and more meetings taking place each week, and, frustratingly for me, my rivals were notching up the winners.

I got placed on a novice chaser for Fred at Chepstow and then when it was expected to win next time out, we got beaten and finished second. A run of seconds and thirds continued until my season eventually started with a win at Worcester and soon afterwards I rode an old almost white chaser for Anne Finch to win at Uttoxeter. I thought things were looking up again; I was mistaken. Fred sent one of his most promising novice chasers, Bolus Head, up to Wetherby for a Wills Qualifier. I felt a big responsibility on my young shoulders and pre-race nerves got to me a bit. All appeared to be going quite well and I was enjoying the power that this young horse was showing but quite unexpectedly he landed awkwardly two out and I had to pull him up. I jumped off immediately and found the poor horse had broken his shoulder. Fred was very upset as he had high hopes for the horse and unfortunately he put the blame squarely on my shoulders. He was adamant that I had jumped into the back of the horse in front and that the horse's hind leg had caught Bolus Head on the point of his shoulder. I had never disputed Fred's view and in my own distraught state this was not going to be the first time, although I have never believed his version of events could have been correct.

It was another long, miserable drive home. I had another hurdle race winner for the yard the following week and got placed on Double Negative, who was going to become quite a friend. On the following Saturday Brown Admiral was set to run at Kempton and we had a few at Warwick so it should be a good weekend. On

Friday morning Fred told me that he knew that I would be disappointed but he felt that, as John was the senior jockey, he really should ride Brown Admiral and I would go to Warwick where he expected Lewis to win the handicap hurdle. I was disappointed as I did not want to lose the ride on the Admiral but at least I had a good chance of a winner at Warwick, although I had never ridden Lewis before.

Riding out that morning I got wind of a bit of a gamble being planned on Lewis. He had shown great form at the back end of last season when John had won on him twice and Fred and Mercy felt that he was still well handicapped. I knew I had to do the business and once more I was feeling the pressure a bit. Fred always liked his jockeys to get a good start and jump out quickly from the starting gate. 'Free ground,' he would say, 'make the most of it lad, jump out and take a pull into a nice position.'

Lewis could take a fair hold so I thought it best not to jump out quite as quickly as normal, but from then on things began to go wrong. I was never able to find a nice position in the race and was uneasy throughout the early stages. Also, as it was only two miles, we were going very quickly, and I was only just holding my position. Down the back at Warwick, with five flights left to jump, Paper Rich and Jeff Pearce kicked for home and went clear, so I pressed the button to follow but with little effect. Four lengths down on the inside turning for home with Master Davenport going well on my outside I was boxed in and made a fatal decision, one I wouldn't have made if I had learnt the lesson Bobby Coonan tried to teach me four years ago around Fairyhouse. I decided to go up the inside of Paper Riche, thinking that taking that short cut was the only way I was going to win. As Paper Rich weakened I got upsides him as I approached the second last flight, but Jeff pulled his horse over to close the gap and Lewis and I went flying out through the wing. Thankfully the wing was made of modern splinter-proof plastic and it broke up without causing us to fall. Master Davenport went on to win by five lengths from Paper Rich with the rest of the field well beaten. I had a very sore knee which I must have caught on one of the two upright posts in the wing but Fred had no sympathy and understandably blamed me for taking the route I did. The stewards laid the blame firmly on Pearce and banned him for ten days for dangerous riding. This was no consolation to me as I was going to be off for longer with a damaged knee and I had got beaten on another fancied Rimell mount.

I got back to Plot 9 to be told by Nigel that Fred was planning on selling our house and he thought he might go and take his two horses over to Kim and join him at Brackley. The good old days were certainly over but perhaps this was my chance to really concentrate on my career, get properly fit, think about my diet and make a move to try and get on some of the best horses in training at the time. It was my chance to reach for the stars and I was going to give it my very best shot.

After riding out on Sunday morning I knew Fred and Mercy were in their office on their own so I suggested to Nigel that this was an ideal time to go and tell them that he was leaving and to get it over with now. He agreed and went along to give them the bad news. He was only there five minutes and promptly came to tell me that they wanted to see me now. My knee should be in good enough shape by Saturday so I assumed we were going to discuss riding plans for the following weekend, which we often did on a Sunday morning. I went in full of the joys of spring and Fred asked me to sit down, but the atmosphere was not good, which I assumed was due to the news of Nigel's departure. Before I had time to draw breath Fred uttered the words that changed my life: 'Nigel's moving on and we think it's best if you go as well.' I was absolutely speechless and the contents of my stomach turned to water as I took in what he had just said. 'Mercy and I do not think that you are experienced enough for the job and you will not be riding any more for us. Perhaps when you are more experienced you can ride for us again in a couple of years' time.'

I left their office that Sunday in November 1977 with my life in tatters. From dreams of stardom, I had no job, nowhere to live and I was a long way from home. My mates in the yard politely expressed their surprise. Nigel, although concerned that his decision had somehow precipitated this move, was his usual light-hearted self. He knew where he was going, but I had no idea which way to turn let alone where to go. Joining Nigel at Kim's yard was a route I would not consider, and running back to Ireland was treated with similar disdain. I was going to see this through on my own if necessary. I did not return to ride out for Fred the next day, but instead I was on the telephone searching for opportunities.

I wasn't sure which way to turn but I certainly was not going to give up. I had already tasted considerable success and deep down I knew I could compete with the best of them, but how was I going to get on another horse let alone a good one? I spent a long night trying to work out what had gone wrong. I had got beaten on a few fancied runners but I had had a couple of winners as well. Bolus Head was a disaster but I was convinced that was an unfortunate accident caused by the jar of landing on fast ground rather than any collision. Lewis was certainly the straw that broke the camel's back, or was it? Kim had gone and now Nigel was going as well, Fred wanted to sell Plot 9 and I began to tell myself he thought a clean sweep was the easiest solution.

We had been a noisy bunch on the gallops, we had larked about without a care in the world in the yard and Fred and Mercy had had enough. They saw us as a gang of three and they would get rid of us as a gang of three. If only Fred had taken me aside, given me a strict talking to and told me where my race riding was going wrong, things could have been so very different but Fred was never one to do things by half and he thought a harsher lesson had to be learnt. 'You can ride again for me in two years' time,' was a crumb of comfort that was going to keep my flame burning through some dark and lonely moments.

In those days all the main racing stables had their own jockey, and some had two or even three. I decided that I would try and get a job at one of the big yards in the area, and David 'the Duke' Nicholson was the obvious choice. He had been a very successful jump jockey himself and had now transferred his attentions to training with considerable success. He was also known, like his father Frenchie, for bringing on young jockeys. Unfortunately, as far as I could see, he had four if not five jockeys working for him already, so I decided that there was little point in even asking him. Whether he would have taken me on or not is a moot point, but if he had I am sure I would have got the tuition I needed, but then of course I probably did not think I needed any tuition.

The other trainer in the area who trained a fairly large string was John Edwards who had just moved to a new house and training yard near Leominster. I decided to give him a call; if I had known what I was going to go through at the time, it would have taken more guts than it did, but without much further thought I took the plunge. Many times I was to wish that I had thought more before I jumped, but jump I did into muck, sweat and tears which I only escaped from by nothing short of a minor miracle.

Still trying to keep hold of some respectability, perhaps in recognition of my expensive education, I offered my services as an assistant trainer rather than a second-rate jockey who had just been fired. No flies on John Edwards, regardless of what I saw myself as, so he took me on, no doubt as a stable lad who would at least be able to ride the difficult ones if nothing else.

I arrived up at Aymestrey three days after being told to go from the security of the Rimells, with no more than a suitcase for all my belongings. Gina, John's wife, greeted me while trying to do a dozen different jobs at once and also looking after two small children. The house was hectic, the yard a bit of a mess compared to what I was used to and there seemed to be hardly any staff to look after a mass of horses poking their heads out of any excuse for a stable. I could see why he had taken me on without asking too many questions. I was quickly told the rules and what was expected of me and finally if I was ever fortunate enough to go to the races to ride for someone else, my wages would be deducted, adding: 'The way you ride I don't suppose you will be away very often.'

I was told I was sharing lodgings in the bungalow at the bottom of the drive with James, who turned out to be a quiet lad from Cork, and two girls, one of whom had come down all the way from Scotland, and somehow this was a crumb of comfort. I got into my car leaden-hearted and went down to investigate my new home. There was hardly room to swing a kitten, let alone a cat, the kitchen was filthy and my bedroom smelt damp and mouldy. Wall Cottage was bad, although at least it had a bit of charm, but this place had nothing and it matched my mood at the time.

Thankfully my fall from grace had not caused Penelope to run off looking for better prospects. We had to travel a bit more and my car put on the miles but any distance was never too far. London nightclubs now stretched my limited budget a bit too far and quiet dinners for two became the bright light to look forward to at the end of a long week. Impressing my girl with a bottle of Blue Nun was, I thought, the best way to start a romantic evening; thankfully being a wine connoisseur was not one of her many qualities, and it certainly was not one of mine. However, the intensity of our love could not be maintained and by the end of this difficult winter I found my eye was wandering elsewhere and in the spring I committed a fatal blow to a magical relationship.

The small trainers that I had been riding for did not cast me aside and naturally I made sure they knew I was keen to ride anything, anywhere. I always had the belief that however difficult they were to ride, however hard they pulled or however badly they jumped I could ride them and, as far as I was concerned, once at the start in a race I had a chance of winning on them, whatever the odds. Despite this setback that I was going through, and others that came along right through my career, I always had that belief and thankfully on many occasions it paid great dividends, while also resulting in some heavy falls.

On one of my first rides back, almost a month to the day after leaving Fred, I won a novice chase on Sure Enough at Nottingham, trained by Mrs Courage of Spanish Steps fame, beating into second place one of the Rimells' better horses. It was a sweet victory and one that I savoured. It took a couple of months before I rode any for my new boss and when eventually I did, although no winners, thankfully nothing went badly wrong. His stable jockey was Philip Blacker, who is now a famous sculptor, but Stan Mellor had first claim on his services so there should be some opportunities if I could gain favour. Christmas came and went and I had a few rides at Wolverhampton, my usual Boxing Day haunt. I got one placed but no more joy. Colin Tinkler had taken my place at the Rimells' and was making a very good job of it. However, at least I was now supplementing my income from working in the yard with quite a few rides and I was doing my level best to pull myself back up the ladder. John eventually showed enough confidence in me to allow me to ride his smart Flat race recruit Lighter in a novice hurdle. He had won first time out at Leicester with Philip and was odds-on to do so again. Thankfully he did just that.

Cheltenham and Aintree came and went, with memories of the fun of playing a small part in those big occasions dominated as the days passed all too slowly by. I persevered trying to get an ounce more ability out of any of the largely low-rated horses I was lucky enough to get my leg over. I was beginning to get a few more rides and the occasional winner came my way. I was riding a few for my old mate Kim and won on a wonderful old chaser called Flap belonging to his mum at Windsor. On Easter Bank Holiday Monday, I had six rides in the afternoon for the first time. None of them won but at least totalling up my riding fees of £36 a ride added up to quite a good day's work.

Later in May, Kim decided to make a foray up to Hexham with three of his horses, which meant a fateful weekend in Northumberland. We fancied Flap on the Saturday but I managed to fall off him, and Jamie Butchart rode his other one that afternoon which ran well enough but we still had one to run on the Monday so we planned to party over the weekend. A little new blood from the south was a good opportunity for the local female talent to ensure we had a good time and that was just what we intended.

In the midst of it all I met Annabelle, the daughter of a local estate owner, and she was certainly ready to party. To make matters worse I had a sore head and a little tender loving care was too big a temptation to turn down. We were well looked after and had a great weekend. I had found a new friend whom I was sure I would see again. We left Northumberland without any winners but the weekend made a lasting impression on me, and this was going to have a very big impact on my life in the years ahead. In the end I had three more winners before the end of that eventful season. I was grabbing all the opportunities I could, both with two legs and four, but I was not always thinking of the consequences.

Previous summers had been spent enjoying the warmth of success with time away for nearly six weeks, pampered at home in Ireland and then the beautiful west coast of Mayo to enjoy, but my situation was different now. I was now a stable lad, albeit riding in a few races, and holidays were few and far between. I only managed a week away and then it was back to looking after the growing number of horses that John Edwards was acquiring. I put my head down and got on with it in the hope that I would find favour and get on some of the better horses rather than those which no one else wanted to ride on the racecourse.

As the season got going I once again felt the pangs of envy as other jockeys started to pile in the winners. I did have one ride in August which finished second and then had a winner in September but rides were few and far between. In November I was pleased to get the ride on Anne Finch's good two-mile chaser Grangewood Girl and we ran well to finish second.

Soon afterwards John and Gina put me up on their smart young chaser Good Prospect, but unfortunately we were second again. It was not until just before Christmas that I rode Good Prospect again and this time won on him at Stratford. All the time I was watching Fred Rimell and his two jockeys John Burke and Colin Tinkler provide a continual stream of winners, some of which could have been mine. I was doing my best to bump into Fred now at appropriate moments, congratulate him when he had a winner and occasionally remind him of his promise on that dark day over a year ago, 'perhaps in two years' time'.

I had a lean Christmas, which had previously been a very productive time for me and thin pickings remained my diet throughout the winter. I had further humiliation after having had the news that John wanted me to ride Lighter in the Erin Foods Champion Hurdle at Leopardstown which was a rare chance for me to ride in a televised race. I arrived over in Ireland with the horse and looked after him overnight, only to be told before racing started that Tommy Carberry had become available and was now going to ride him. Mum and Dad had travelled up from home to watch the race only to be greeted by a pretty dejected son. He did not finish in the first three.

I had no rides at Cheltenham, although our yard had a winner when Lighter won the Stayers' Hurdle under Philip

Blacker. Things looked up for me when a week before Aintree Ginger McCain asked me to ride my old favourite from the Rimell days, Brown Admiral, in the National. It was great to be part of this wonderful occasion again and I felt a glimmer of hope that my career might get back on course. This, however, was not going to be the occasion. The Admiral went well for a circuit and then, as he was tiring, we had what is often called a misunderstanding and I rather unceremoniously fell off. Rubstic was the first Scottish winner of the race for some time that year in a race where thirty-four started and only seven finished. It was not long before unwarranted hysteria hit the racing pages from the Animal Rights crew, as cries of cruelty and massacre at Aintree hit the racing pages.

Over the next five years we were to see a considerable change to the shape of the fences and the challenging drop at Becher's Brook was removed entirely. The Grand National remains the greatest jumping race in the world and modern splinter-proof plastic wings and railings, along with good turf management have made it as safe as any other race. Horses love the challenge just as much as the jockeys, but they enjoyed it just as much before the steamroller of our nanny state began to take its toll. The race is now considered safe enough to run the best chasers in, and the old-fashioned jumping type is unlikely to get a run, let alone win. That rules out so many of the recent winners – Rag Trade for one, Last Suspect another, there are scores of them – and Red Rum would never have been rated high enough to get to the starting gate. It is run at a faster pace and long-priced winners are most unlikely, but whether these are improvements is a matter of opinion. I think you can guess mine.

That spring, John and Gina and their considerable entourage moved to the grandeur of Caradoc Court on the banks of the Wye between Hereford and Ross-on-Wye. John, as well as being a good trainer, was never slow to see an opportunity and as far as I could gather some serious wheeler-dealing had taken place to ensure he could secure this substantial property. Caradoc Court was big, some might call it a pile, others would love it. It was set in lovely old gardens with an extensive walled garden and three hundred acres of farmland with numerous small woods and coppices. It was a sportsman's playground and John was going to make the most of it. He loved his shooting and high pheasants were guaranteed. The River Wye still had a reasonable run of salmon and he had three-quarters of a mile of single bank fishing with a number of named pools and the local hounds were only kennelled just up the road. I liked the sound of all this as well, but there was an awful lot to do to get the place ready in order to turn it into a successful training establishment and we still had thirty-odd horses to look after.

We were only a small team and we had to turn our hand to everything. Naturally I said driving a tractor was no problem to me so rolling the gallops was one of my many jobs after riding out three or sometimes four. One gallop was straightforward, straight out of the drive, across the road and up and down the gallop, piece of cake. But having managed this without disaster I was then told to take the roller to the bottom gallop and do that one. This meant going half a mile down the road round some very tight bends on a steep incline. It was not long before I found myself being pushed out of control down this steep hill due, I guess, to the unexpected weight of the large roller I had on behind. I had not worked out all the gears I had at my disposal and it was very hairy to say the least. Thankfully no traffic was coming, as the consequences could have been more than a little serious. With my heavy roller doing its best to overtake the tractor, somehow we got to the bottom still together and on the road in one piece.

One near miss rolled into another. Four lots to ride, tired and hot at lunchtime I rode out a young stallion without a shirt on. As I got off to open a gate he suddenly snorted and lashed out a front leg at me, another snort, rear and paddle both front legs in my direction, there was no chance of me getting back on, so alone and some distance from help I tried to lead him back to the yard. I was sweating in the heat and I could see he was aroused, but the smell off me was making things worse. Suddenly he lashed out and knocked me to the ground, and as I lay flat on my back I saw his white bared teeth coming straight down at me. He tore into my arm and chest, I kicked frantically at his head and thankfully connected sufficiently for him to let go and with a large snort he galloped off up the lane towards the nearby field of mares. I arrived back in the yard to be greeted with panic. I was obviously looking far worse than I was, although I was in quite bad shape.

My top half was covered in blood and I had a deep wound on my left arm. The young stallion, who was showing signs that he might win a hurdle race, had gone back to wild instincts and I was lucky to only require some stitching where he had bitten into and through my bicep muscle on my upper arm and some dressing of cuts on my chest which was lacerated. Thankfully he had missed my face. Unfortunately, the muscle in my left arm was left permanently damaged and there were bad moments ahead when I had to let my arm dangle loose in a race to restore the blood flow and allow reasonable service to continue. I was, however, lucky to escape more serious injury and I can still see those white teeth coming at me today.

That summer passed quickly. I had little time on my hands and I was determined to do all I could to ensure my painfully slow rise back to being a jockey with a full-time career ahead of me and not some sort of 'jack of all trades' at home in the yard; able to turn my hand to a lot of things but good at very little was a painfully true description at times. Slightly out of the blue, my freedom as no more than 'one of the lads' in the yard came to an abrupt end when Annabelle came down from Hexham to work as a cook for the boss and his family. We promptly moved into one of the gatehouses on the estate and for the first time since leaving home four years earlier I had found someone who wanted to, and more importantly was ready to, look after me full time. I enjoyed the many benefits and soon fell into a happy routine. We were good together and we had fun.

The season once again got underway at Newton Abbot in August and, much to my surprise and delight, John put me up on one of his first runners in a novice hurdle. We finished down the field but at least I got my name in the papers as a jockey and hopefully other rides would follow. They were sadly few and far between, with no more than a couple of rides throughout August and September; promises ahead but I had had them before. Then towards the end of October a thin ray of light gave me renewed encouragement. John let me ride his wife's smart little chaser Good Prospect up at Carlisle. It was a long way to go and the pressure was on to make it worthwhile but the little horse was fit and well, and thankfully we won.

Soon afterwards Pamela Sykes, who had been an owner with Fred and Mercy, put me up on one she was training herself from the Welsh Borders and that won at Hereford. Fred was there and in his usual magnanimous way was full of congratulations for us both and I was feeling brave enough to remind him of his promise two years earlier that one day he would put me up again. A smile and a wink told me he had not forgotten. Into November and I was briefly back on the big stage as John and Gina allowed me to keep the ride on Good Prospect in the Hennessy Gold Cup. Under bottom weight we finished midfield, but the day improved when I was second on a nice young horse for Mrs Sykes, Royal Commotion.

I picked up odds and ends through the rest of November and December, riding about once a week on horses that I always managed to think had a chance of winning, but in reality others had to run pretty badly to let me near the winner's enclosure. Boxing Day at Wolverhampton was going to prove an annual Christmas celebration for me and 1979 was no different. John put me up on a good-looking but one-paced young chaser called Again The Same and we won with something in hand, and Royal Commotion ran well but was second again. However, this proved only a brief respite from the drudgery of long drives to ride horses that very often had little chance of winning and invariably were not very safe conveyances. I was at least getting to the races but I was desperate to get myself established again.

Then out of the blue on the evening of Thursday 24th January 1980 I got the telephone call I had been waiting for, for over two years. 'Sam, Fred Rimell here, I want you to ride one for me in the novice chase at Cheltenham on Saturday, it's called Cheltenham and it will nearly win, so I'll see you there.' I put down the telephone as if I had been hit by a thunderbolt. I had hoped it would happen and had a secret feeling it would, but in reality I knew it was very unlikely. I simply could not believe it and at the home of jump racing this Saturday; I was intoxicated. I rang the Press Association immediately and told an equally surprised reporter to put my name beside one of Fred's horses for the first time in two years. He congratulated me. Annabelle was as excited as I was and the pub beckoned for a celebration supper.

A Gateway to Heaven

ANNABELLE AND I went to Cheltenham together. I had the two rides that afternoon, although one of them meant more to me than all the others I had ridden over the last two years. Jockeys in those days always wore a jacket and tie to the races, while my best suit gave the impression of confidence and a young man going places, but underneath the butterflies were already beginning to spread their wings. I got the usual nod of welcome as I passed through the weighing room where that day's Jockey Club officials were doing their final preparations for the day ahead. The Clerk of the Scales was checking jockeys' likely weights to see if any riding today looked as if they had expectations to ride at weights normally below their limits and the immaculately turned out Stipendiary Stewards were busy researching the previous form of some of the talking horses of the day, while the two starters mused about the quality of their lunch, a bit better than the day before seemed to be the general impression. Lunch was not on my mind.

The friendly atmosphere of the changing room was a welcome hiding place. My mates knew exactly how I felt and to a man they were congratulatory on my sudden and unexpected call up by Mr Rimell. Some of course

were soon to point out that in their opinion my mount
had next to no chance and they would not want to ride
the thing anyway but it was all good-natured stuff and
this usual humour was not going to dent my confidence.
I was going out to give this horse the ride of my life,
even if, as I had now noticed, it had indeed fallen quite
a few times in its short racing career. Fred said it would
nearly win and win it would. I hid behind the *Sporting
Life*, although checking the form of my opponents was
not something I did very often, but it was a good way to
pass the time and at least I looked relaxed.

A lot of excitement in the *Sporting Life* that morning
centred around Fred's runner in the last, Swashbuckling, and this reflected in a definite buzz in the changing
room. This was not centred on my reappearance on
board an apparently unreliable novice chaser but about
Peter Scudamore's new partnership with Fred and this
very exciting prospect they had in the last. Swashbuckling, who had been a very expensive purchase earlier in
the year, had bolted up first time out over hurdles, and if
he passed the test this afternoon he was bound to be all
the rage to win one of the big hurdle races coming up in
March at the Festival meeting. It meant little to me, but I
had my toe back on the bottom rung of the ladder and I
knew I had a long way to climb before and if ever I could
enjoy those dizzy heights again.

My ride in the first ran well, finishing just behind
the placed horses, so I was pleased to be safely back in
the weighing room. As the novice chase was not till the
second last race, I settled down to try and relax watch-

ing the rest of the day's racing on the television with my mates in the tea room. All was going much as expected until the fourth race when one of Fred's other runners, Royal Gaye, took a heavy fall. Peter Scudamore was put on a stretcher and came back in the ambulance. Nothing unusual about that as the first aid personnel at the fences and the ambulance crews took every possible precaution to ensure our wellbeing, and thankfully more often than not their exemplary approach was not necessary. However, as is often the case, news of a serious injury filters back to the changing room before it goes anywhere else. 'Scu is hurt and won't ride again today,' whistled around our benches like a lit fuse on fireworks night. 'Who will ride Fred's in the last?' was the immediate response around the room.

With only a slight interest in the result of this debate I listened to the senior boys tossing the idea among themselves. A lot of them had rides in the race but were already weighing up the consequences of getting off their intended mount to make themselves available, and those mutterings were certainly coming from Jeff King, a champion jockey in all but name. There might be a chance to get on quite a few of Fred's high flyers in the weeks ahead now that Scu was on the sidelines. Grasping any opportunity that arises, even if it was to the disadvantage of others was a vital part of a jockey's precarious existence. Francome and Andy Turnell were making noises that they maybe could manoeuvre things their way.

A large man suddenly filled the door of the changing room and the excited chatter was replaced with the nervous silence of a classroom of schoolboys caught sneaking a look at the next day's exam papers. It was Fred, and he looked around the room and then, much to my horror, he pointed a finger at me. In his authoritative tone he beckoned me over. 'Come here Sam,' was all I heard but his next sentence was going to rock me to the core. 'You will ride ours in the last and it will win. Pull up the bugger in the novice chase as quickly as you can; it's a dangerous bastard and we need you in one piece.' I went back to my place with butterflies hatching quicker than mayflies on Lough Mask on a sunny May morning. Soon they had all taken flight and a visit to the loo was the only answer.

My mates were full of a mixture of envy and excitement. Some probably thought with me on Fred's hotpot in the last they had a bigger chance of winning it themselves whereas others knew the torture I would be going through, hoping I could produce the goods. I went out to ride Cheltenham in the novice chase, feeling an inch or two taller, because if Fred and Mercy thought I was good enough to ride one of their best I must be OK at this job I loved so much and, with no pressure to win on this one, I was going to have some fun before the big test. I jumped off in front, getting a clear view of the big stiff Cheltenham fences on this dodgy jumper and set the pace according to my wishes and the horse's ability and not the ability of others. Landing over each fence safely was a pleasant surprise and after completing a circuit I was still in front; as was so often the case I began to have the feeling that perhaps I could win this race after all. Expectations continued to rise as we rose the hill on the far side of the course prior to the final gallop down towards that long pull up to the winning post and then 'Snap!' – my reins went to the buckle, all momentum was lost and we went from first place to sixth in half as many seconds but thankfully we were still on our feet. I agreed he was indeed a dangerous bastard and I obeyed Fred's instructions, pulling him up immediately. Job done, now the real business of the day loomed large and the swarm of butterflies were once again practising manoeuvres in a pretty small space.

I went back into the den of the jockeys' changing room and tried to look as calm, cool and collected as I possibly could. Thankfully there was now little time to sit and think, as it is always a rush to change colours and sort possibly a new saddle and almost certainly a new weight for the next race. I am sure my mates knew how I felt but I was not going to give them the chance for a practical joke or two as that would certainly make matters worse at this particular moment. Tom Buckingham had the well-known yellow and black colours ready for me on my peg and I felt very privileged as I put them on for the first time. These colours were always associated with quality and they had been in the winner's enclosure at Cheltenham many times before. My weight was much the same from my last inauspicious spin so Tom produced the same saddle and we checked the weight – 11st 10lb was required. Fred and Clifford were waiting for me in the weighing room and, having got the nod from the Clerk of the Scales, Fred took the saddle himself with a nodding wink. He knew how I felt and he was a little nervous himself, understandably. Mercy was not smiling much in the parade ring but for a change I did not let this get to me. I had a look at Swashbuckling, and he looked magnificent – stood out a mile – and his lad, Ben, was quite rightly as proud as punch walking him round.

The bell went, Swashbuckling was pulled in and Fred legged me up with his customary good luck wish. This horse was something else to sit on; he oozed quality and cantering to post felt like a Rolls-Royce. I had a good position in the race and he jumped well. I challenged at the last and with a hard-fought battle up the hill we won by a head, from a good young horse trained by Fulke Walwyn, ridden by Bill Smith. Those few inches passing the line were going to change my life. Ben was delighted, and Clifford had had faith in me, backing him even at the short odds he was, and I tried to be as matter-of-fact as I could coming back into the winner's enclosure to be greeted with warm smiles all round and a pat on the shoulder from Fred.

Out of eight rides over the next fortnight five of them won. John and Gina allowed me back on Good Prospect two days later at Chepstow and he won with something in hand, and I then found myself at my lucky course Wolverhampton where Fred had asked me to ride one of his in the first. We got up to win by a hard-fought neck, and this was the first half of a double for me that day, Good Prospect winning again providing the other half. Back there again on Monday with another double, a long-priced winner for Gordon Price and my change of luck was underlined when, after finishing second on Spartan Major for Pamela Sykes, we got awarded the race in the stewards' room. Jeff Pearce, who had put me through the wing causing me to lose my job at Kinnersley some two and a half years earlier, had ridden the winner but this time he had fallen foul of the stewards and was placed last. Someone out there was helping me.

My confidence was sky high, and somehow that confidence must have been flowing down the reins to my horses. Another ride, another winner for Fred soon followed, another for Gordon Price and then on Saturday 6th March, off to Hereford where three of the four horses Pamela Sykes had on the go at her yard near Bishops Castle were running on the same afternoon. Her youngster Royal Commotion won the first by six lengths, her small tiger Bambers Security flew around the sharp two-mile course and won the handicap chase and then, despite hitting the last hard after taking up the lead two out, her precious Straight Cash won the novice chase. Three quarters of her string winning at one of her local tracks, a great training achievement in itself, and ten winners for me since that magical telephone call only a month before – what a difference a day makes!

With the Festival now only ten days away, all heads were turned towards Cheltenham. Pamela was hoping Royal Commotion would be well enough handicapped to warrant running him on the final day of the meeting in the two-mile handicap hurdle, but that appeared to be all I had. I was still on cloud nine so this sudden lack of action did not matter too much to me. My boss John was running two of his horses that I had won on recently and Jim Wilson appeared to be riding them both; he was entitled to think a more experienced jockey was needed for the big occasion. Then out of the blue Fred was on the phone and told me that I could ride Another Dolly in the Champion Chase. 'It will be a good experience for you lad,' was his passing shot as he put down the phone. I was thrilled, and a butterfly swooped from deep in my gut.

Driving rain swept the Cotswolds and Cheltenham came up heavy, so each and every race of the eighteen over the three days was going to be a real test of stamina. These were conditions that invariably suited those from across the water and indeed it was not long before the Irish were singing in the rain. They won the first, second and fourth, although the big one, the Champion Hurdle, was a reverse, when Sea Pigeon, under a peach of ride from Jonjo, beat the heavily-backed Irish favourite Monksfield. Good Prospect, who had given me such fun during the winter, won the Kim Muir on that first day so John and Gina were in celebratory mood.

The yard was in high excitement the next morning and after riding out two for them I set off to have 'a spin' in the Champion Chase, the big race on the second day. The rain had stopped but the ground was still heavy. Chinrullah, trained by Mick O'Toole and ridden by Dessie Hughes, appeared certain to win and, as Fred had already pointed out, I was just there for the experience. For a change I did not feel the slightest bit of pressure and tucked in behind the other seven as we set off at a speed faster than I was used to. Another Dolly was only small but he could jump and jumping kept us in touch until we clouted the first down the back on the final circuit, and at this point Chinrullah began to go clear. He was all of ten lengths clear at the top of the hill and I was at the back of the following group. I heard big Ron Barry shout across to his mate: 'Come on Jonjo, we had better go after him.' Not me, I thought, as I was going too fast for my liking already and I didn't fancy those two downhill fences a single stride faster than I was already going. So I sat still and let them give chase. A gap of four, five then six lengths soon appeared, and I just hoped to finish with some respectability. I met the second last spot on and got a good jump. However, with only one to jump Chinrullah was gone. He was going to win by a distance but suddenly I saw both Ron and Jonjo pick up their whips, and they were going nowhere. Dramatist and Bill Smith were also beaten, so I had a glimmer of hope. I pinged the last and clawed my way past tiring horses to force a photograph for second place on the line. Not fancied, in fact hardly trying, and my number came ringing across the loudspeakers as having finished second. Fred and Mercy and Mr Urquhart, whose colours I had carried that day, were all smiles and I had had another good day. Tied Cottage and Tommy Carberry were placed first in the Gold Cup – although they subsequently lost the race to Master Smudge due to the discovery of a prohibited substance – and before the lights had dimmed that night at Cheltenham the focus moved to Aintree.

Once again I was being swept along on a wave of excitement, and Fred had asked me to ride one of his four runners, Godfrey Secundus, in the big one. I had ridden big Godfrey once before; he was a big, tall horse and, although one-paced, he could jump, so I was already giving myself a great chance. The day before, on the second day of the three-day Aintree meeting, I had a more serious job on my hands. Fred told me I was to ride Western Rose in the big two-mile chase. This was one of the best horses in the yard and was shaping up to be one of the best two-milers in the country; win on this one and rumour had it that I would have the top job with Fred and Mercy next season.

The Mildmay course at Aintree was my sort of track, a front runners' track, sharp and tight with decent fences. Jump out quick, ping your fences and you had a good chance of winning; that was my philosophy anyway. Western Rose loved to stand back and jump and that day he was on song. I was at my best, we won by ten lengths, and that win on the big stage meant a lot to me. To cap a great day I was greeted by the news in the changing room that Chinrullah had been found to have had prohibited substances in his food and had been disqualified from his big Cheltenham win a fortnight earlier. Another Dolly and I had won the Champion Chase, having been very fortunate to get up and be second just on the line – what a result and a real bonus for my now surprisingly healthy bank account.

National morning dawned with the mist rising off the Aintree turf. As part of the Aintree build-up Fred, who had the best training record in the race, liked his runners to have a short canter on the course as dawn was breaking, and today was no exception. This was always fun and a bit special, as there was a wonderfully exciting atmosphere. The press were out early, photographers keen to get a nice early morning shot and a few keen punters who knew where to be on Grand National morning. Godfrey felt well, and I was on a serious high even without this, the biggest adrenalin buzz of all, an occasion when, in the fast lane, a jockey's life is hard to beat. I was not the only one who fancied Godfrey and we started at relatively short odds of 20/1, but we could never go the pace and despite jumping well we got outpaced and I had to pull him up after Becher's second time. The race was won by the American amateur Charlie Fenwick on Ben Nevis, trained by Tim Forster, and one of Fred's runners The Pilgarlic, who was going to become an Aintree specialist and this time was ridden by Ron Hyett, was third. No glory in the big one for me but I went home down the M6 with new hope for my future and not underestimating the quite significant pay cheque I was going to get at the end of the month.

My feet had hardly touched the ground since that magical call from Fred. The number of rides I had had increased almost tenfold, with some of them running well above expectations and a lot of them winning. Questions began to be asked about who was going to be the Rimells' first jockey next season, and rumour had it that it was between Peter Scudamore and me. I must have been still riding in the clouds as I remember thinking that after I had had so much recent success for them, how could they possibly be considering this young jockey, who had only just started to ride some winners, before me. He rode a bit deeper than me, indeed he had longer legs, and you could see he was determined in a finish but he was not nearly as tough or brave as me – that is what I thought anyway. Besides, he had not been at the game long and was at least two years younger than me. I was, however, very excited to be considered for one of the top jobs, if not the best first jockey job in the country at that time. I was not to know my rival was to become one of the best jump jockeys ever, being champion eight times, including a shared title with John Francome (although Francome sportingly stopped riding in 1982 to allow the injured Scudamore a share of the title). Fred was indeed a good judge.

The one big meeting of the season that was left was the Scottish Grand National meeting at Ayr, and invariably the ground had started to dry out when this meeting was usually held in the third week of April and this year was no exception. I was there for the first time enjoying the atmosphere of another big occasion. Fred was running Western Rose in the big novice chase on the second day of the meeting and he had asked me to also ride a highly-thought-of young horse called Gaye Chance, who was getting the reputation of being a bit of a tearaway, and his owners John and Mary Curtis were keen to see if I could get on with him. It was great to be back on Western Rose as he was bold and brave and he had done me such a good turn at Aintree; despite only sitting on him that one time I was already fond of him. It was a high-class field, we hit four out, the first in the straight at Ayr, and this did not help our cause but you could throw a blanket over four of us as we passed the post; I was, however, the one in fourth place. The general mood was that he had run up to expectations and was perhaps ready for his holidays. The night life in Ayr did not tempt me that evening and while others partied I had an early night. I knew I had to at least try and give the very best impression, as my future was under discussion. Late the following day Fred legged me up on Gaye Chance, who had a surprising light mouth for a tearaway, and he took some handling on the way to the start, but during the race I got him buried among the other runners and he settled well.

However, despite starting favourite, we got beaten into fourth place, but I felt I had ridden him well as undoubtedly he was a very difficult ride. Fred must have been satisfied though and before I left Ayr that evening, standing just outside the weighing room that was to be my office ten years later, he told me he would like me to come to Kinnersley in the summer and be his first jockey next season. From the depths of despair eighteen months ago, little more than a faint hope of climbing back up the ladder and so often instead slipping down a twisting snake to the bottom of the pile again, I had now burst out into the sunshine. The sort of opportunity that only a few are fortunate to enjoy had been offered to me on a plate. I was to learn soon afterwards that Peter had in fact been asked by Fred and Mercy to be their jockey but he had turned it down, preferring to stay loyal to David 'the Duke' Nicholson with whom he had had nearly all his success to date. Being second choice did not cause me a flicker of apprehension or indeed disappointment. I had to pinch myself that this was really happening.

Annabelle and I decided we could enjoy this together and we got married in Hexham Catholic Church, although I had been christened a Protestant, and so, as is customary in these situations I had to agree that any children we had would enter the Catholic Church; I just went with the flow as expected. The service was followed by a lavish party at Langley Castle which was situated in the heart of Annabelle's father's estate on the slopes of the South Tyne Valley. After that first brief bit of nookie while somewhat concussed after a fall at Hexham, our love life had blossomed and Annabelle was keen to look after me when I came home from a tiring day at the races. She was the apple of my eye and, being the eldest daughter of the owner of a considerable Northumbrian estate, there was fishing on two lakes and a section of the South Tyne, where there had recently been considerable improvement in the runs of both sea trout and salmon, and pheasants were everywhere. It was indeed quite a sporting paradise ripe for development at a later date.

The Stuff of Dreams

KNOWING THAT I needed to be on parade at Kinnersley in the first week of July, Annabelle and I had our honeymoon before we got married, so once the celebrations were over I was ready to focus entirely on riding winners. We moved to a three-room flat in a wing of an old rectory in Colwall on the western slopes of the Malvern Hills. Although the flat was small it was ideally situated, only fifteen minutes from the Rimell yard, and it was owned by friends of Mum and Dad who were still living in Ireland but would soon be moving back to the West Country to be near their family in England. We had a friendly and very obliging landlord.

I rang Fred to tell him that I was back from holiday. There was no need to hide my enthusiasm and it was easy to make all the right noises about being keen to ride out and get fit for the season ahead. 'See you on Monday, first lot out at eight as usual; with a bit of luck we are going to have a few running early so get yourself running up those hills,' was his cheery reply. Not sure about running up those hills, but I did appear on the first Monday in July for first lot. I was a little intimidated by the reaction I got on my return from two years' absence; it was mixed to say the least. There was evidence of at least two camps among the lads, nearly all of whom had been with Fred when I was part of the team three years earlier. The winners that I had ridden during the last two months of the previous season were sufficient to ensure a favourable welcome by the lads who had been involved in those successes. I was grateful for their support and indeed enthusiasm as there was definitely evidence that a portion of the team had hoped that the young Peter Scudamore had got the job. It was fairly plain that they saw him as a better road to riches than a once-tried Morshead. I also found evidence of a small fire and some loyalty still burning for John Burke. However, Fred was firmly on my side and how I benefited from that.

This time round there was no formal walk around the yard with Fred introducing me to all the horses as he had done when I first appeared for work as the stable amateur four years earlier. He knew that I had seen most of his string running during the previous season and had been fortunate enough to ride a few of them already. It was soon clear that the daily routine had not changed at all. Monday was a gentle day with only a few having a steady canter and most horses were off round the roads for a good trot. My responsibility was soon to dawn on me when I began to take in that not only the five that cantered that first day but also the forty-odd others being taken round the roads in three long strings that morning, were all mine to ride over the coming months.

What an exciting bunch they were. There were some new faces but my old favourites Western Rose and Swashbuckling looked fantastic, as indeed did all the others.

Where it all started, although this picture was taken a bit before my time. The Meath Pony Club camp.

Practising already? Buffy was gentle.

Being beaten by the master of his day Ted Walsh was no disgrace. Navan 1974.
Strange Delight was fun.

Getting beat by Tuscan Prince and Keith Brown at Sandown in 1975 was still a thrill.
Iceman was cool.

Above: A spectacular jump on the outside, one of many, on the way to winning the Greenall Whitley at Haydock in 1976. Royal Frolic was a star. *Below:* Safely in mid-air (far left) but about to crumble on landing in the 1981 Grand National, Brown Admiral was consistent.

A moment of real pleasure passing the post in front for my first Cheltenham Festival winner in the 1981 Royal & SunAlliance Hurdle. Gaye Chance oozed quality.

On the way to winning at Hereford soon after a long period off through injury in 1986. Karnatak had springs in his feet.

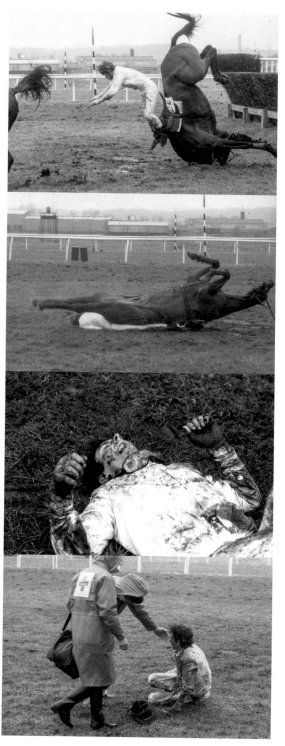

A right good
burying at Newbury
in 1985. Three
Point Turn was
well named.

Unceremoniously ejected from the saddle in the 1982 Grand National.
Pilot Officer was clumsy at times.

A rare tranquil
moment at
Cheltenham in
1982 with Laura
and Clifford.
Pirate Son had
the Rimell stamp
of quality.

The black and gold colours of Pamela Sykes for whom I was fortunate to ride a lot of winners. Spartan Major was tough.

Racing at Perth on a summer's day with the new Nelson stand in the background. I loved Perth and my team.

Celebrating my retirement in the middle of my cancer treatment. Left to right: John Francome, Steve Smith Eccles, myself, Peter Scudamore, Neil Doughty, Hywel Davies, Steve Charlton and Paul Barton. They are great mates.

Top: Finally, a big one. Without the best boatman it would not be possible. John Maye is the best. *Middle:* Happy with this one. Jonathan Ruck Keene looks on. Altnabrochy Lodge in Co Mayo was heaven for me. *Bottom:* Sue on the West Coast of Scotland in happier times.

Some were still fat from their summer holidays but from small and neat to big and rangy they all had the stamp of quality that Fred and Mercy were now famous for. Not for a second did I feel daunted by the challenge ahead, and my confidence was sky high. Fred would train them, Ron Peachey, who was still in place as head lad, would feed them and keep them well and Mercy would place them in the right races plus Johnny McConnochie was the ever-reliable assistant trainer and we got on well; all I needed was a little luck and they would all win.

Fred was true to his word, and ten days before the season was due to start at Newton Abbot on the 2nd August we had one to school over hurdles and two to school over fences. I always found schooling mornings at Kinnersley a bit nerve-racking and this first one of the season was no exception, I knew I had to perform up to expectations. As usual Mercy was there, sitting firmly astride her grey hack Bucket. Fred gave the instructions and I just hoped Mercy had no cause to open her mouth until we were safely back in the yard and the merits of various horses could be discussed in a more temperate climate. North Yard was fast and furious, a classy four-year-old who had shown some form on the Flat. I knew he would be keen but, although he was a bit rapid over his hurdles, he showed plenty of scope and there was general contentment all round.

Keithson was only small but a nice neat little number to sit on and he cantered down over the three fences in Deer Park as if he had springs in his feet; I was going to enjoy this one. Wareath was not so straightforward –

keen, awkward and not appearing to give much thought to anything other than galloping as fast as he could in any direction. However, when pointed in the right direction he could jump, thank goodness. All the babies had been given a good lead by Allied Carpets who knew the game well and was the ideal schoolmaster for this occasion. Eddie Woods, whose father Paddy Woods used to ride Arkle, had ridden him and was the stable amateur at the time. No need for any post mortem, the morning had gone without a hitch and we were ready to rock and roll.

On the second day of the new season on my first ride back, North Yard bolted in at Newton Abbot, and two days later Keithson won his first novice chase at Devon and Exeter. At Worcester on the Saturday of that first week, Wareath also won and North Yard bolted in again. Four rides and four winners in six days. Back at Worcester eight days later Allied Carpets won, Keithson won and North Yard won again, my first treble. It was all too easy. North Yard was to run once more that first month, winning again at Newton Abbot. We had had eight runners from the yard, I had ridden them all and they had all won; at the end of the first month of the season Fred was leading trainer and I was leading jockey. This was the stuff dreams were made of and importantly any disquiet among the lads had been firmly dispelled. My first season as stable jockey carried on in this remarkable vein. Gaye Chance won his first hurdle race at Stratford in October followed by progressively more testing wins at Cheltenham and Worcester. Western Rose won at Ascot on the same day as one of the old stars in the yard, Connaught Ranger, won at Newcastle with John Burke in the saddle. Mercy was notably pleased to have found a good winner for John and for the first time I was aware that while Fred's support was always immense, the other side of this formidable partnership still had to be fully won over. There was one further fly in the ointment during this near-perfect start to the season – Swashbuckling had to be taken out of training.

However, Mercy continued to place our runners with great skill, and wherever they ran they were expected to win and mostly win they did. Three runners, three winners over two days at Haydock was followed by a double at Cheltenham. One of these was a successful reunion for the season with Pamela Sykes, who now had a nice small string for me to ride, whenever I was not needed by Fred. Trying to dodge annoying clashes or worse still going to a different meeting to her runners was a continual challenge which tested my skills of persuasion. Two winners over the Boxing Day Wolverhampton meeting brought my winner tally to twenty-eight. Only a handful of our runners had not been winners, and we had had a couple of seconds and only one faller. I took it all for granted. Fred was one of the best trainers in the land and he had some of the best horses who were put in the right races and I had to steer them round.

Fred liked his horses ridden much the same way each time. 'Ride your nice race, and be lucky lad,' were always his parting words as he legged me up. He liked me to jump out in front at the start – 'free ground so make the most of it' was his motto. He liked me then to take

107

a pull and drop in on the rail third or fourth, keep them switched off as long as possible, switch them on and take up the lead at some point after the second last and go on to win. I rarely had to worry about the other runners. I never studied the form book – there was no need as far as I was concerned as I would get the very best out of my mount and with any luck they were better than the opposition anyway. It was all very straightforward and I lapped it all up as it was all meant to happen this way.

In the second week of January a big white van drew up at our gate and on confirming my name and address the driver started to unload a number of large boxes marked 'Fragile'. This had been hinted at before by my mates in the weighing room but I could not believe it – I had won the Waterford Crystal award for riding the most winners in December. One hundred beautiful Waterford Crystal glasses had indeed arrived. By chance I had ridden eleven winners in the month, one more than the chasing pack.

My strike rate hardly dipped in January and February although we had fewer runners than during the run-up to Christmas, which was the way Fred liked to run his yard. The big prestigious races of the season were now looming. Gaye Chance went to the valuable Philip Cornes Final at Newbury in the first week of March, still unbeaten after five runs. He started at 11/1, led at the last and won by two and a half lengths in heavier ground than he had had to cope with before and on his first run over three miles. This felt like my first big winner for the yard and a new milestone had been achieved. Gaye Chance and I now enjoyed a good rapport. I knew he had a terrific turn of speed and he was quick and economical over his hurdles. He could also really stand back which suited me and as long as I could get him to relax early on it was going to take some smart horse to beat him.

Ron Peachey was just the man to take care of this little jewel. Three miles in the mud at Newbury must have taken its toll and with only ten days to Cheltenham a minor miracle was needed. Ron hid him away for seven of those days, I certainly never saw him, but a cheery wink from his devoted lad Phillip was enough to tell me that all was going according to plan.

The papers were now full of Cheltenham stories – who would win the Gold Cup and the Champion Hurdle, what the big Irish fancies were – but thank goodness Gaye Chance never got a mention. His target was the Sun Alliance Hurdle, the opening two and-a-half-mile hurdle race on the second day and this was to me the most important race I was ever to ride in but to most it was really no more than the aperitif before the bigger races later in the afternoon. It was quite enough for me knowing the whole yard fancied his chances and it was my job to deliver. The damp weather continued during the week, so Cheltenham was sure to be on the soft side or softer, but I was happy enough with that. Fred asked me not to take any rides from outside yards in case I got injured. On the Thursday before the big week all four of our Cheltenham horses did their final bit of work down in Deer Park where I rode Gaye Chance and he felt as good as ever.

We had no runners on the first day of the meeting but I went along to absorb the atmosphere and have a good look at the track and conditions. Horses were indeed finishing tired, the Irish runners were in form and I watched a great duel in the Champion Hurdle with Sea Pigeon coming with a very late run ridden by John Francome and getting up to win on the line. One of many brilliant rides by the champion jockey.

Annabelle and I arrived before most of the traffic on Wednesday, as the last thing I needed was a rush to get ready. Instead I had a long wait in the changing room; it was a good place to be. Plenty of chat about yesterday's winners and losers, some gas about what some of the boys had got up to last night and the inevitable debate about what would win today. I did not want to show my nerves and kept fairly quiet. Whilst I was now firmly a member of the band of jockeys that travelled day to day from meeting to meeting, I was well down the ranks. When I arrived in England and had my first ride at Towcester some five years earlier, my peg was right at the bottom of a long line of pegs that snaked their way round the walls. Gradually, as I rode more winners, I moved slowly up the pecking order, and I was about halfway now but today there were at least ten jockeys up ahead of me. Jeff King was at the top peg, his great mate Andy Turnell sat beside him, then there was John Francome followed by Bill Smith. Up from me were two of my best mates, Hywel Davies and Steve Smith Eccles.

Eck and I were born within twenty-four hours of each other and it always amused us that whilst Eck was the son of a miner and his home was in a small Nottinghamshire mining town, I had, as he would say, been born with a silver spoon in my mouth and enjoyed a private education, but we regularly fought it out in mud, rain, snow, and drought for that matter, on the racecourses of the UK, trying to make a living doing exactly the same thing. Time would prove that he was by far the better jockey, but at the time I needed to feel that I was as good as anyone out there and I did. Despite the supposed 'silver spoon' I had been brought up tough and as far as I was concerned those days that were cold and wet and miserable were the days that I had an advantage. I loved riding in the mud and rain.

The bell signalling the jockeys to get ready rang out and, finding my blue and gold silk cover for my crash helmet, I grabbed my whip and went to queue for Tom Buck to tie my silk tight over my helmet and put the rubber bands over my wrists to keep my sleeves tidy. Butterflies were now grouping in my stomach and I needed to get going. I wasn't superstitious about being out in the parade ring first but I liked to be first as I thought it just set the tone of intent and I was first out into the cauldron of excitement that afternoon.

The parade ring was full, brimming with hopeful and expectant owners and trainers, and the rails were packed six deep with eager punters desperate to get as close to the action as they could, ensuring a good look at their fancy. As I walked out I felt I could cut the atmosphere with a knife; this was as good as it could get. Fred and Mercy, John and Mary Curtis, Gaye Chance's owners, John McConnochie our assistant trainer and Clifford Rawlings, the trusted travelling head lad, were there in a tight huddle. They were keen to get me safely aboard and away to the start; their job was now all but done, the rest was up to me. Almost as soon as they greeted me, the bell to mount went immediately. A few brief pleasantries, as no one was in the mood for pre-race chat. 'Be lucky lad, ride your nice race,' as Fred patted me on the back and legged me up. It might well have been a selling hurdle around Exeter. That was part of Fred's magic. He knew I was nervous and this calm, everyday approach had the desired effect. I relaxed as we went off down to post, past stands packed like bees in a swarm; I was going to enjoy this.

My friend underneath me felt good too. He was keen and I wanted to conserve as much of his energy as possible, so there was some mild disagreement about what pace we should go, but it was time for a compromise and not a fight. Walking around at the start in the centre of the course, it was soon obvious this was no Exeter seller. Not the usual muttering of who was going on, who wanted to be handy but much more muted than normal, and not much was being given away. The mere hint of the starter going to his rostrum and twenty-two horses and jockeys turned in the same direction pushing their way into their chosen position.

'Hold on jockeys, hold on,' roared the starter as he climbed his rostrum. 'Come on now, get your head back off the tape,' he yelled. With that he roared 'Come on then,' and the tape sprang away and we were off. I had got myself into the position I wanted and jumped off behind the leaders on the inside, but the pace was much faster than normal and, despite jumping the first fast and well, I was soon back in about seventh place. We were very tightly packed round the bottom bend, although I was nicely on the rail, before turning up the straight for the first time. Jumping the second there was more than the usual crash and clatter as hooves and fetlocks crashed through the top rail of the neat birch hurdle. I did not see but on the outside there had been a faller and he had in fact brought down Dunaree, the favourite and the best-backed Irish horse in the race. I was concentrating on what was going on ahead of me and immediately beside me. No chatter now, as every bit of concentration was needed; giving an inch could mean being shuffled back in the field, and any error would mean the end of the dream.

I picked enough light at every hurdle to ensure my high-spirited friend could use his powerful jump to his advantage, without having to change gear and switch him on to racing mode. We held our ground and, as others fell away around us going up the hill, the leader was eight lengths ahead and looking around there were about six horses left with a chance. As they quickened down the hill I was forced to ask for an effort and much to my joy I felt a response. Moving into fourth we pinged the second last and fought for third place on the long sweeping bend for home, and with a quick smack from my whip and another surge of power, I was gaining on the two ahead. A length down at the last, my whip was up and we pinged it; Gaye Chance had it in him and we surged by them both. Halfway up the run-in, heads down, all whips flying, we fought for dominance. A huge surge of relief and excitement rushed through me as we passed the post one and a half lengths ahead.

My mate Hywel, riding Bee Sting, was second and he was the first to congratulate me. Phillip, Gaye Chance's very loyal lad ran down the course with a smile splitting his face, and Clifford followed flushed with excitement. The walk back through the car park around the back of the weighing room gave the three of us a few moments to enjoy the moment in peace and then that magical drop into the winner's enclosure and natural amphitheatre. I had done it. Those dark days, the sack and two years in the doldrums, were well behind me now and I had delivered on the biggest stage of all. Fred and Mercy were delighted. 'Well done Sam,' another big pat on the back, and John and Mary Curtis were ecstatic. I was bustled back into the weighing room, with the scribes from the press desperate for a word, so there was not enough space and time to enjoy the moment. The senior Clerk of the Scales weighed me back in with warm congratulations and I went back into the hectic throng of the changing room to be greeted with genuine back-slapping from the vast majority of those within. Both John and Tom Buckingham knew what it meant to me as well, rather like a good ghillie when their student catches their first salmon or shoots their first stag; they show more pleasure than the lucky recipient. It was great to be among friends to share the moment.

I had another ride for Fred that day in the Coral Final and Wait And See with his jockey somewhere in the clouds ran a blinder to finish second behind an easy winner, Cheltenham specialist Willie Wumpkins, ridden by another Cheltenham specialist Jim Wilson. It was then time to party with Gaye Chance's owners and enjoy Fred and Mercy's company, all of us in the very best of form. The world and his wife appeared keen to congratulate me and they were moments to savour before we left Cheltenham late that evening.

The following day I came down to earth with a bit of a bump. I had one ride, again for Fred, in the County Hurdle, a fast competitive race over the minimum distance two miles. As always I thought I had a chance and it materialised that way as I turned into the straight with one flight to jump on the inside with only four or five in front of me. With no running rail I took what looked to me the shortest route on the inside between the last two hurdles but somebody coming from behind thought different and went to go up my inside. Whether it was memories of the lesson Bobby Coonan had taught me round Fairyhouse some years earlier, or me just feeling still on a high from the day before I don't know, but my competitive edge certainly got the better of me and I deliberately pulled little Albion Prince over on top of him and stopped his run. My horse had run out of steam and I soon went backwards so it was a pointless exercise and the stewards took an understandably dim view of it and gave me five days' holiday. Fred was not amused and I hate to think what Mercy thought of it. Still Cheltenham had been fantastic for me; a few days' rest was not a concern at the time.

The first major test of my career was behind me, success was now being rewarded with monthly pay cheques above my wildest dreams, Kinnersley was buzzing with excitement and Fred was full of smiles and cheeky tales. We all went to Liverpool and the Grand National meeting full of more expectations. Surprisingly we had nothing in the National but John Edwards had asked me to ride Son And Heir for him, so I was looking forward to that. In the first race on Grand National day I had my favourite Western Rose in the two-mile handicap chase. He loved the sharp Mildmay track and I loved riding him there. In front of a huge Grand National crowd he beat the odds-on Anaglogs Daughter by eight lengths winning in style. He was like a king that day and proved himself to be one of the best two-milers about. Son And Heir ran well for a circuit in the big one and then tiring going out on the second circuit he refused at the nineteenth, the first big ditch on the second lap. I ended up with my face planted into the firs on top of the fence, having been ejected at a speed faster than I could handle.

That was one slight shock, but I had another one coming. Annabelle and I had been back home about ten days when we got a call from the manager of the Adelphi Hotel in Liverpool asking me to pay for the room service we had had on the eve of the Grand National. Knowing we did not have any room service I asked the manager what this was for. 'A case of champagne, £499, and you have signed,' was his reply. I was of course astounded, this was going to take some explaining to the Mrs. In desperation I asked, having denied any knowledge of this, if he would please send me the invoice. Much to my relief he said he would. My memory was bad but surely I would have remembered this extravagance. We waited nervously for this bit of post to arrive, and two days later the letter came, so I pulled it open to examine the contents. Room 241 – that was our room – a case of Bollinger £499, and in desperation I looked at my signature. The chancer had spelt Morshead wrong, putting an extra 'e' in the middle. What a relief! I rang the manager and he could do nothing but accept someone had ripped them off and thankfully it was not me to pay. Some punter had no doubt thought I should pay for his losses.

This magical season had yet one more pinnacle. There was one more valuable prize to be won at the mixed meeting at Haydock at the beginning of May, the most valuable handicap hurdle of the year. Gaye Chance seemed well, a remarkable training feat in itself, so we went to post one more time with seven unbeaten runs under our belt in a very competitive eighteen-runner two-mile handicap. We were outpaced a bit early on but made steady headway up the straight, hitting the front after the last to go away and win by four lengths. His eighth win of the season, becoming the first horse to win over £100,000 in prize money in one season, and he was to be awarded the distinction of Best Novice Hurdler for the season. He deserved a good holiday and with the ground now beginning to dry out Fred quickly shut up shop for the season. He had plans for next year and thank goodness I was now firmly in place to enjoy those with him. I had ridden sixty-two winners and was fifth in the jockeys' table. I was included in the invitation to the Ritz Club in London where the top five jockeys were presented with nice cheques by Max Kingsley, chairman of the Ritz Club, prior to dinner, followed by a night on the roulette tables; we had an amazing night.

Changing Times

MY SUMMER BREAK was interrupted by the shock news that Fred had died. News of his illness was sparse, and I certainly had no idea that it was life-threatening when Annabelle and I, with our new baby, had set off up to Northumberland to spend some time at her father's estate in early June. Checking this year's lambs was for Annabelle like a bee to a field of distant clover, very hard to resist. I could not believe that this larger than life character had been taken from this world so suddenly. The funeral was a mammoth affair, and the small church in Severn Stoke was bursting at the seams with a huge array of racing's dignitaries and, of course, family and close friends. This was no celebration of a great life and a great man as in normal circumstances it would have been. To a man we all felt that we had been robbed of a treasure trove that had so much more to give. The devastation that cancer causes was not so prevalent then as it is now and the speed with which Fred's life was taken away made the loss even harder to bear for all of us, not least Mercy and his close family. The least I could do was to get across to the yard, ride out and prepare for the season ahead, as in early July the horses were just starting to come in and it had to be all hands on deck.

On the back of a good season I had invested in a nice farmhouse and outbuildings with a small paddock for the pony just five miles from Kinnersley. It was sold under the hammer while the roads were covered in snow as the main lot in a local auction. I put myself into the bidding ring very late after a slow start, and thought we had it at this early stage but suddenly it was obvious that someone else wanted it as badly as we did. I did not let up and it went up in £2,000 bids by £26,000 in a few fraught seconds, increasing its value by a quarter. I thought I had it and was not going to lose it now, but when it was finally knocked down to me it was way above my budget. Thankfully it proved to be a great buy and a happy home.

The bathroom was big enough to fit a sauna which was the first job to be done, as I needed to keep my weight down. Almost every evening of my racing life I had a sauna. I found it easier that way, as losing a pound or two every day allowed me to eat as normally as I could. That meant a slice of toast and tea for breakfast, a cup of tea and a small sandwich at the races, if I was not doing light, and normally a small but quite normal supper, then the sauna. Today's dieticians would have something to say about that plan. On one occasion I got as hot as I could in the sauna then dashed out to roll in a snowdrift and then went back up into the sauna to get warm again, whereupon I promptly fainted as the sudden change of temperature was too much for my system. That was fun but not the ending I expected.

It was inevitable that Kinnersley would not be the same without Fred. Everyone missed him; the smiling rock was no longer there. However, the big ship was still afloat although with a new captain at the helm, but no one knew whether this ship would remain on course or worse still not stay afloat. John McConnochie was still on hand as assistant trainer thank goodness and he took up some of the slack, while Ron Peachey, in typical Guards fashion, buckled down to the job in hand. I think we were all slightly nervous of Mercy, and I am afraid to admit that I think I was frightened of her even at that very early stage. The lads remained loyal to the cause, as winners for them meant bonuses in their weekly pay packets. My place appeared safe enough, although I knew that I was going to have to manage without my main supporter, someone who understood race riding from a jockey's perspective and who could provide a balanced view in the face of defeat. My own father had died only six months earlier and now I had lost another father figure. Advice from an elder statesman was something I was short of and something I was certainly going to lack in the future. I was swimming in rough waters on my own.

As the start of the season drew near I felt the tension begin to rise, and early results were going to be vital. The sporting press were keen to make copy on Mercy taking up the training licence in her name, one of only a small handful of lady trainers and none with such a big string at their disposal. I was not the only one who felt that this particular lady, doing a man's job, was not going to hide behind her feminine qualities, and she was more likely to step up to the plate where some men would fear to go.

Straight Line was our first runner but he needed the run quite badly. Nothing else ran until his second run at Worcester two weeks later, where he was leading two out before he fell, when looking like winning, at the last. Not good. I was OK and promptly got the leg up on Tru Mar in the handicap hurdle. Raceform reported: Always prominent, disputed lead from two out, hard ridden to lead flat. That was how much it meant to me. I desperately wanted to win and win we did, Mercy's first winner. Straight Line also won easily next time out at Hereford; we were on our way.

To ease the pressure I was already putting myself under, I had by now thankfully built up a small handful of trainers who were keen to use my services. John Spearing and Pamela Sykes had some horses ready for an early campaign and winners continued to flow both at the early West Country meetings and nearer to home. Three doubles in October kept my name in the news and I was entitled to feel my career was on course for even greater things. Gaye Chance was quite fat for his first run at Worcester and was only fourth in a moderate race but he went on to win the Tom Masson Trophy at Newbury and I steered a new little star in the yard, Gaye Chance's half-brother Gaye Brief, to his first win in a poor novice hurdle round Hereford. A bad run of seconds then began to upset the applecart. Both Western Rose and Gaye Chance just got beaten in good races round Kempton, with Gaye Chance running a blinder but just failing to get up to finish second in a very competitive Mecca Bookmakers Handicap Hurdle.

The excitement was such that Annabelle started labour pains soon after driving away from the races and we had to stop off with relatives in Bedford just off the A1, and our first child popped out in Bedford Hospital before midnight. The excitement of the birth of my first son soon pushed the disappointment of these defeats into the background and my next ride was a novice chase around Nottingham which we won. Winter was soon to strike and a host of meetings were abandoned due to a run of cold weather with snow stretching right across the country. With a small baby at home and some winners under my belt, the loss of most of the Christmas programme, including my happy hunting ground at Wolverhampton, was not a worry to me. I kept fit by riding out three or four mornings a week, but it was an ideal time to switch off and enjoy family life.

Pirate Son, one of my favourite horses, kept things ticking along with a nice win at Cheltenham and, when the weather improved halfway into February, Gaye Brief showed his class by winning a Panama Cigar Qualifier at the next Cheltenham fixture and the Rossington Main at Doncaster, whilst Gaye Chance won the Champion Hurdle trial at Haydock. Others from the yard won as well and both Pamela and John Spearing were doing their bit to help my bank balance; all or nearly all was going well. The winds of change came when Scudamore beat us into second place riding St Alezan, who had been moved to Martin Tate from our yard at the beginning of the season. It was the first prick of a poisoned thorn and Mercy's mood began to change dramatically. It was a painful defeat, not one I was going to be allowed to forget, and on top of that, perhaps because I was now trying too hard and little thought was going into the art of race riding, we had another bad run of seconds and some falls. Thankfully that was halted by Mercy using her skill at placing horses to perfection, who found the ideal race for Gaye Chance, allowing him to hack up in the Balmoral Hurdle at Doncaster, an ideal prep for his bid for the Champion Hurdle in six weeks' time.

I was not going to see Cheltenham. In the first week of March I went to Newbury for two rides, one of which was Celtic Rambler in the novice chase. I was not looking forward to him, although I had won some good hurdle races on him and indeed one around Newbury, as he was not a natural jumper – clumsy and heavy-headed with precious little scope. We might have won a competitive handicap hurdle around this good galloping track but his chasing career I knew was more suited to easier courses like Worcester and Wolverhampton. I told my mates in the weighing room that this one was not one to be trusted. However, once on board the usual drop of adrenalin soon transformed fear into the will to win and by the time we got to the start I had already made a sound case for forthcoming success. We went well enough for a circuit and a half, then as the pace quickened we were found wanting and while trying my utmost to hold a prominent position turning out of the back straight, we met the cross fence all wrong and somersaulted to the ground.

Worse was to come, when John Francome and his well-fancied mount, with nowhere to go, ran straight into the prostrate Celtic Rambler and had no choice but to fall over the top of him. He then proceeded to do a forward roll, his horse's head using my chest as the springboard. The champion jockey did have a few fancied rides that day and all I remember of this unfortunate occasion was John coming over to me and telling me what a bloody fool I was in fairly choice language. Luckily for me his anger drifted by in waves of nausea, as those stalwarts of National Hunt racing, the first aid men, crowded round.

The next thing I knew was that I was in an ambulance with its siren blazing, and with Kim Bailey who had kindly agreed to keep me company. I was a bit short of breath and had the usual headache, but what was all this fuss about? I was soon to find out. Taken by the hand into Basingstoke Hospital, a white-coated doctor appeared with a sharp, V-shaped blade in his right hand. 'We have to do this to save your life, don't worry it won't hurt,' and with that he stuck it straight through my rib cage into one side of my chest cavity. I had a collapsed lung and this was the necessary treatment to save the situation, apparently. Whether I passed out then I am not sure but the next few days were a blur. I understand now that Kim was asked to keep me awake for two hours to ensure that I didn't go to sleep. Fortunately he is a good talker. When I was conscious enough to appreciate what was going on I found that I was on a life support machine and had tubes coming out of most of my orifices.

After a couple of days I was conscious enough to recognise my visitors but the only way I could communicate with them was to scribble cryptic notes on a pad of paper kindly given to me by the nurses. Annabelle and Charlie, our four-month old son, came down to stay nearby and she was able to come in twice a day, thankfully leaving the baby behind. Pamela showed her concern, driving down from Shropshire, dropping in as regularly as she could, and I remember the dismay she showed when all I wanted to know was what winners I was missing. Some of my fellow jockeys came in to say hello and try to cheer me up. Francome, who was always good at making us all laugh, was one of the first of them, although his humour caused yet more pain in my rib cage. However, it was not an environment he liked or indeed was used to and the state he found me in after his brief outburst, when I was prostrate on the ground, caused him some embarrassment and shock rippled across his anxious face.

I was two weeks in hospital, and dreams of Cheltenham glory had faded early. I was pleased to be back home to watch the mud-splattered battleground from my own bed. I had to watch Peter Scudamore take over most of my rides from Kinnersley, enough in fact to have a serious impact on the jockeys' championship that year, sharing the title with John Francome in the end.

It was, however, Jonjo who I watched get the leg up on my little hero Gaye Chance in the Champion Hurdle with more than a little trepidation. Not surprisingly, despite my loyalty to his owners John and Mary Curtis I did not really want him to win, as missing winners was one thing but missing winning the Champion Hurdle was quite another. Sadly for them he did not run anything like up to expectations. It was good to hear that Mercy was fuming with someone who was far more skilful than I was ever going to be but I wish her wrath slipped as easily off my back as it did from Jonjo's.

However, watching results unfold over the coming weeks became more and more difficult, as Kinnersley began to hit a purple patch, and the darling of the day was Peter Scudamore. He was now beginning to show his genuine expertise. Under the guiding hand of his boss David Nicholson he had become not only a very polished jockey but a strong one as well. He sat very quiet on his horses during a race, appeared to get himself into a challenging position with little effort and then moved into overdrive at the vital moment, just like a sparrowhawk diving streamlined in for the kill.

On a Saturday afternoon in May I watched Chepstow on the BBC, where Scu had three good rides for Mercy, and all were warm favourites. One after the other they won like odds-on shots and Mercy's smile got bigger and bigger as the day wore on. Gloom descended on me like a cloud of grey smog. This was exactly what I did not need. Each day dragged as the season slowly wound to an end. Scu was now well and truly the golden boy, and I was going to need a lot more than two healthy lungs to climb back to my place on the ladder, let alone push him off his perch.

I was up and about as the season drew to a close but regaining full capacity in my shrunken lung was a long process. I found running torturous at the best of times, but now it was positively painful. I should have spent time swimming but that involved shelling out a few quid each time and that was enough to put me off. Pushing the pain barrier seemed a less painful option. I did make time to drive round and see the handful of trainers that had put me up during the previous season and also began to ride out regularly at Kinnersley. Mercy appeared happy to see me and was without doubt glad that I appeared to have made a full recovery, but she was not slow in telling me how much success she and Scu had had together at the end of the previous season...a marker had been thrown down.

By the time the new season came round again I was desperate to get back on the racetrack. With all those winners while I was on the sidelines Mercy was now even more aware that she did not need me. However, I still had favour with the majority of her owners so I started again as her stable jockey. There was nothing from the yard to run early on so once again I was left a free hand to chase all the rides I could from other trainers. Ken Bridgwater rang me for some of his and I built a quick rapport with a tough little hurdler called Tabernacle. He had terrible legs and was not much more than a plater, but he tried his heart out and we got on well. His will to win very nearly got me in deep trouble one afternoon though when, having passed the post in front and won, to my complete amazement I was asked to walk past the Clerk of the Scales and fail to weigh in, thus getting myself disqualified. A large chunk of cash was on offer, but thankfully, despite my income being seriously curtailed over the previous six months, I turned the offer down without giving it a second thought. It was the only time I witnessed real skulduggery in twelve years of race riding and in my present position as a racecourse manager there is not a year that passes without me thinking how fortunate I was not to weaken to temptation on that summer's afternoon nearly thirty-five years ago.

I was now riding out quite regularly for Jim Old and winners from his yard and from Pamela once again got me through to October when the season started to get into full flow. I had five winners in August so things were looking good and they continued that way, and a 20/1 winner for Mercy was a boost for our working relationship. The good horses were beginning to come on stream. Mercy was short of young horses but some of my old favourites were still there and my mate Western Rose got things moving with a good win at Kempton. One new star by the name of Very Promising was showing his undoubted quality on the Kinnersley gallops and he gave me a great ride to bolt in first time out at Uttoxeter. I felt the pressure a bit that day, as expectations were high and I knew we had to deliver. Gaye Brief soon followed first time out and beating Scu on a good young horse of David Nicholson's in the Tom Masson Trophy at Newbury was a big relief.

The rivalry between our two yards was getting more and more intense. For his next run I had to travel all the way to Huntingdon for another valuable conditions event; it was a long way to go to get beaten, but thankfully we didn't. Mercy put Scu up on Celtic Isle, one of my favourites, on the same day at Newbury and of course he won. The pressure was on again with Gaye Chance having his first run over fences in the Fred Rimell Novice Chase at Worcester. He had schooled well at home and his class meant all he had to do was jump around safely. Thank goodness, despite being a bit backward, he did just that and Mercy walked tall, all smiles. Three weeks later he was sent all the way to Newcastle but once again a long trip was worthwhile and he won quite easily. Surprisingly that was going to be his last easy win as things proved more difficult for him as the season progressed.

I was still having a good time and riding winners for a lot of different trainers and some good wins for Mercy included two novice chase winners on Connaught Ranger, a horse with a lot of talent but not the easiest of rides. Gaye Chance came up against another rising star in Combs Ditch in a Lambert and Butler Qualifier at Ascot. We jumped to the front two out expecting to go on and win but from nowhere Colin Brown and Combs Ditch appeared and flew by us as if we were standing still. Mercy was dumfounded and could not understand how I had managed to get this class act beaten. Future form was going to suggest that while the ease of victory was surprising, we had met a good horse on a good day. Thankfully I was soon back where I wanted to be in the winner's enclosure and winners continued to flow through December, including a three-timer at my lucky track Wolverhampton, two for Mercy and one for Pamela Sykes. Pilot Officer, my future ride in the National, won at Haydock and Very Promising won again. I was flying.

In mid-January I thought I was going to ride my first four-timer, all for Mercy. I had three in the bag and in typical bravado manner and expecting a little more than was possible in asking my little horse Sarsfield to jump to the front two out, he clipped the top and gave us both a crashing fall. A great day was ending in the ambulance and another rush off to hospital, this time with a suspected ruptured spleen. I was a little concerned with this news as, although I had the now customary headache, I did not feel ill at all. However, the duty doctor told me that I must stay in overnight and that unfortunately I would have to be disturbed every hour to measure my stomach as any change in my girth would indicate trouble. 'If it is burst you can bleed to death in an hour,' was his parting shot as he said his goodbyes for the night. Matter-of-fact it might have been, but those informative words did nothing for my sleep pattern. After the best part of fifty minutes trying to get to sleep, just in my ninth minute of finally getting some peaceful dozing an attractive little nurse would come and wake me. Instantly wide awake I would watch her face as she wrapped a tape measure around my waist, her smile remaining fixed on her pretty face, and I relaxed again knowing my 32-inch waist had not suddenly become one of 36 inches.

This process went on until 2am, when a new, rather older nurse appeared. Once more, suddenly wide awake, I watched her face, expecting boredom to remain predominant within her dull, tired expression. A streak of anxiety crossed her eyes and my heart leapt into overdrive. 'What was your previous measurement?' she asked. By this time, in my mind, I was down the corridor into the operating theatre with a ruptured spleen. She measured again and looked at me for an answer, looking even more concerned. 'Thirty-two,' I said as calmly as I could. 'Oh that is all right,' she said, 'I was measuring from the wrong end!' It took a while for my heart to stop racing and each hour I went through the same ordeal, but thankfully no more hiccups with the tape measure and without further ceremony I was allowed home the next day, spleen in one piece.

As it turned out it would have been far easier and quicker if the medical team had taken Mercy's advice as she apparently told anxious friends that she had seen me pee and as there was no blood in my urine I could not have burst my spleen. She was astute and knowledge-able in many fields. I had another entry in my medical book but not for concussion, so I rode again at Bangor immediately afterwards. Headaches came and went for a couple of weeks, my lacerated hands, having been caught by sharp flailing steel shoes were sore but with gloves over the top they posed no problems.

Things began to unravel. I was clear two out in the Welsh National on Pilot Officer and got beaten a head by Corbiere. Thankfully the rollercoaster ran back in my favour for a bit with Western Rose, who was sent all the way up to Doncaster and won again and I found myself winning two good hurdle races, the Rendlesham Hurdle for Robin Blakeney on Mellie and the Oteley Hurdle on Cima for Jim Old, and Very Promising won at Kempton.

Down we went again when Gaye Chance was second, beaten three lengths by Fifty Dollars More in the Time-form Chase at Haydock. He should have won as we hit the last fence hard and lost a lot of momentum, which was my fault, so I did not feel good. This was his prep race before Cheltenham and things had now not gone his way on three consecutive outings, not the perfect preparation for our season's main target, the big prize at Cheltenham, and that is where our eyes now began to focus. He was bound to be very well-fancied to win the Sun Alliance Chase and was indeed to start a warm favourite. Mercy had her eye on one nice little prize en route to this feast as Very Promising was off to Chepstow and the Panama Cigar Hurdle Final. Fred had often used this race as a better option for his best novices rather than throw them into the unforgiving Cheltenham battles. Once more it paid off and I enjoyed sweet success with what was proving to be a very special little operator; it was a valuable race to win.

The first day of the Festival got off to the perfect start for Kinnersley when Gaye Brief, now ridden by Sheikh Ali Abu Khamsin's retained jockey Richard Linley, won the Champion Hurdle. It was a lovely performance, despite jumping the last slightly awkwardly, as he quickened away to beat Boreen Prince and For Auction three lengths and seven. Any annoyance of losing the ride mid-season to a retained jockey did not last long, for I was soon swept along with the euphoria of the yard winning a big prize and of course my mind was firmly set on my task the following day.

Whether I allowed this big win to affect me I don't know but I felt under intense pressure as Wednesday of Cheltenham began to unfold. Gaye Chance's high expectations were I found making headlines in every paper; I should have stopped reading them and taken to the usual game of cards in the changing room. These were not butterflies in my stomach, it was more like an army of ants. I did not notice the first two races that day, as I was wrapped in another world hoping that I would be lucky. Luck was again meant to be playing a major role, but I should have learnt years before that skill and judgement were far more important.

My near black athletic friend felt well and on the first circuit we were happy enough. As expected, the pace increased going away from the stands the second time and suddenly the usual gears were not there, and I was losing my place instead of gaining one or two. I had told myself I needed to be close at hand before we had to race down that hill for home, which is a position Fred always advised, and I was not going to be in that position unless something dramatic happened. I picked up my whip and told my trusted friend that he had to quicken now or it was going to be too late. My timing was poor and my approach to the next fence, the big ditch at the top of the hill, worse. I foolishly thought we needed a big jump, but he said on this occasion I was asking too much and took another stride, getting so close he had no chance of staying on his feet. All our dreams came crashing to the ground and a fair weight of Cheltenham punter cash at the same time. The lift back to the weighing room to face the waiting pack of press, Mercy and the Curtis's was the worst of my riding career. I knew I had managed to throw this star to the ground; we might not have been travelling well, but it was an agony I had to live with. I did not notice the rest of the meeting, my world was literally in tatters, or I felt it was.

I was, however, back in the winners early the following week and, amongst another run of seconds, had a winner for Mercy at Ludlow. I had some nice rides at Liverpool to look forward to and hoped desperately to make up for the disappointment of Cheltenham. The meeting started well with Very Promising winning the first race of the meeting; thank goodness for that. It went downhill from there. Gaye Chance got beaten half a length by Everett when starting favourite and Western Rose, back at his happy hunting ground, found one better than him on the day. I had high hopes in the National though. Pilot Officer had shown by his game run in the Welsh National, when finishing second beaten a head by Corbiere, that he could stay the distance and although he was not going to be an easy ride over these bigger fences I knew he had a good chance as did a fair portion of the betting public. We travelled well for a circuit, taking a few fir branches with us as we went, but still in a good position at the Chair we got too low and I was fired unceremoniously into the Aintree turf.

The spring equinox proceeded then to give an unusual amount of rain and a lot of meetings were lost due to waterlogging, including the final Cheltenham meeting of the season. The ground was described as heavy right up to the final meeting at Stratford at the end of May. I did manage a couple more winners before I got a bang on the head and missed Mercy's final runner of the season which won at Hereford. If it was not for the disappointments of Gaye Chance's big race failures and the pressure I put myself under, which probably helped to cause those failures, I had had a perfectly respectable season, just short of fifty winners, including some big wins and some hard-fought successes and for quite a number of different trainers. Mercy and I had had a lot of winners but I was beginning to feel she wanted a different pilot. I needed a holiday and thankfully salmon in the west of Ireland were on the agenda. Annabelle, now quite heavily pregnant with our second child, went back up to Northumberland to mind her flock and I swapped the pain of a rollercoaster of a season for the ecstasy of rising salmon in the golden glides of a spate river in Mayo.

I needed to escape from it all and to me there was no better place than Altnabrochy Lodge, an old shooting lodge situated in the middle of a small meander on the banks of the Brook, the main spawning tributary of the Owenmore River in the western foothills of Nephin Beg. I would always take my car loaded with various rods and reels to cater for all weathers including drought when, with the river not fishable, we would climb down cliffs on the west coast and chase big pollock. My large hairy lurcher Paddington Bear was also a constant companion. The excitement would start often weeks before when discussions on the telephone with my fishing mates on weather forecasts and recent catches would start, and fly tying sessions would get more intense.

I have enjoyed tying my own flies since I was very young. The excitement would reach fever pitch as I crossed the great River Shannon and felt I was at last in the west. Had there been any rain, excitement at the merest puddle? Using the windscreen wipers invariably meant a telephone call to my long-term fishing mate and childhood friend Andrew McKeever, now the senior Turf Club Judge in Ireland, who is a good fisherman despite having 'one glass eye'. It was quite simple in those days, a flood or simply good water in the Owenmore River meant we would catch salmon, and what sport that was.

The Lodge only had electricity in the kitchen – a freezer was the only modern luxury needed – and gas lights adorned the oak-panelled walls, with furniture to match, throughout the other rooms, all oozing fishing tales stretching back nearly one hundred and fifty years. The Brook, the home that hundreds of silver migrants are heading for from late June to October from their feeding grounds in the North Atlantic to spawn, is a wonderful mountain stream and is always a delight to fish in a flood on a late summer's afternoon. Catching a salmon in it is a challenge, although I have been fortunate on a couple of occasions, while a bag of breakfast sea trout is the more likely result. The Brook enters the main river after meandering through a flat peat meadow for nearly two miles at Bellacorick, home until very recently to a peat-fired power station. Two hundred yards down from this junction is the first named pool, Barrack. An attractive run into a productive pool with a good lie opposite the gauge, anything above six inches at this point is nectar, and twenty-five yards down there is an obvious lie behind a big boulder. This is soon followed by Bush or Bushes

– there are three of them – and Black Bank, two glorious pools which speak for themselves and from where epic tales of screaming reels have regularly kept tired fishermen up into the night. Garrawana and Doghera soon follow, given water and a good north-west wind these holding pools are as near a certainty as there is in salmon fishing, split by the excitement of Corrybeg and Corrymore and that is only half of it before the top stretch runs out at Pig. It is all the stuff of dreams as this wonderful peat-stained miracle runs out to the sea seven miles west of Bangor Erris into Blacksod Bay.

I have fished this river with the same group of friends every year for forty years, and never for one moment have I been bored of it or them for that matter. It has been a place of both great healing for me and great joy. Sadly it would appear that excessive netting at sea and regrettably in the river itself is now threatening the continued existence of this river as a holiday destination as salmon are becoming very few and far between and conservation measures have had to be put in place. It might well be only a place of dreams for me now, but there are plenty of those.

On the Downhill Slope

I NEVER MADE time to reflect on previous mistakes, and it never crossed my mind that I should change my way of riding; by doing so my strike rate would surely have improved. To me falls were just part of the job, so I always tried my damnedest to win without a care in the world for my own safekeeping. If winning meant driving all my rides over the last few obstacles as if there was no obstacle there, so be it. Some of the time we would indeed fall over but on many occasions we won, often at long odds, and that was all the reward I was looking for. Once the season got going I was having on average a fall a week, although I did not think this was much worse than any of my colleagues and from the vast majority I walked away unhurt.

Seven years of race riding had not taught me very much, because as far as I was concerned I was as good as the best of them and better than most, but I had just been on the wrong side of the demon luck too often. I continued to try harder and harder, and some would unfortunately tell me how brave I was, but that was not doing me any good as my reaction was often to kick harder and harder, especially when riding for Mercy when the pressure was at its greatest, or at least I felt it was. One skill I had which

I did not appreciate at the time, is that I was a good talker and that probably saved the day on many occasions.

Early visits to the winner's enclosure for my usual stalwarts in August and September were interrupted by the birth of my second son in Hexham Hospital, who was born in clover surrounded by large numbers of Annabelle's family and friends. I left the new member of my family, Harry, in safe hands as I tore back down the motorway to try and increase my harvest around the West Country circuit. Things got underway with a winner in the first week for Jim Old, but Mercy only had one runner early and that got beaten, so by the middle of September I had five on the board. A treble at Bangor at the end of September, two of them Mercy's, put me back in favour for a week or two. The ground remained very firm right into November that year and rides were in slightly short supply, but thankfully my smaller trainers were still providing the goods. Western Rose came out earlier than usual but got beaten at Cheltenham, as his front-running style meant he could never get home up that hill, but then we got lucky winning a two-horse race at Ascot when the other, Artifice ridden by Scudamore, fell. It was a nervous experience jumping all the way round Ascot on our own. I won the Fighting Fifth for the second time on Gaye Brief, getting the ride as Linley was riding at Cheltenham. However, Ekbalco fell heavily early in the home straight which was a sad loss to racing. Gaye Chance ran well, going under by twelve lengths to Brown Chamberlin in the Hennessy, so not too much gloom there. That defeat cannot have been my fault. Wolverhampton on Boxing Day was disappointing but there was some relief with a winner at Newbury for Mercy on New Year's Eve.

My small trainers kept me going and we had fun with one of John Spearing's at Stratford. He told me this one was going to have blinkers on for the first time in the hope it would make him try a bit harder and he reminded me that he would stop quickly if I hit him or even tried to push him out. I devised a plan, a rarity in my riding days. At the start I told all the jockeys that this thing had blinkers on for the first time and would probably run away with me and then stop; so not to worry I would be going far too fast and would soon run out of gas.

When the tape went up I jumped out like a scalded cat and by the second hurdle I was nearly a hurdle clear, so the trick had worked so far. Passing the stands first time they had made no attempt to catch me but my little beast was beginning to curl up and stop. I knew I could not give him a kick let alone hit him, so I grabbed the reins a little tighter so he would feel the bit firmer in his mouth in the hope that he might feel he was indeed running away with me and I began to roar at him. He kept galloping, and thankfully he was a good little jumper. Turning into the straight the others were now catching us fast but with yet more roaring we just held on to win by a neck. I was coming back all smiles to my trainer but blowing a lot. John said to me, 'Why are you blowing so much, are you not fit?' 'You would be blowing if you had to shout at this little monkey for a mile and a half,' I replied. 'Not much good that would have done, I have cotton wool stuffed in his ears,' he said. John Spearing was a shrewd trainer and like me was prepared to try anything.

Mercy then decided that, as there appeared to be a lack of good three-mile hurdlers on the go, she would put Gaye Chance back over hurdles. This did not prove to be immediately successful as we got beaten at Cheltenham, but soon afterwards he won the Rendlesham Hurdle at Kempton with a bit in hand. The Stayers' Hurdle at the Festival was now the obvious target. Thankfully I stayed clear of injury, rode a few winners on the way and went to Cheltenham with a number of rides and high hopes we could atone for last season's disappointment.

Tuesday was the big day for me and it started well enough with Very Promising running well to finish third in the Champion Hurdle, beaten three lengths by Jonjo on Dawn Run. As soon as I jumped off this gem I was soon legged up on my proven star Gaye Chance. This time there was no mistake. The trip was three miles and, making headway to lead after the second last, we held on in a driving finish to win by half a length and the same; neither Goldspun and Scudamore nor Daring Run and Tommy Carmody could get by us. It was with relief rather than pleasure that I made my way back to the winner's enclosure that day. I was not enjoying the big occasions any more. Fleeting relief as I pulled up and then focused on the next problem ahead – the fun had gone out of it.

However, I was soon back on happier hunting grounds with a treble at Uttoxeter, so confidence was high again and we went into the Liverpool meeting in good spirits. I had a late booking by 'the Duke' David Nicholson, to ride Jacko in the National and once again looked forward to Western Rose in the two-mile chase. He ran his customary good race, although this time just getting beaten by Little Bay, given a peach of a ride by the champion jockey-elect John Francome. Jacko gave me a good ride in the big one. Although he was outpaced most of the way, he jumped well and for a change we got round and finished without any hard luck stories. Pilot Officer ran in the race again, this time pulling up, but Mercy choosing to have a different jockey on him, Adrian Sharpe, was another signal to me that things were not entirely rosy in the garden.

The ground dried out quickly that year and John Spearing and Pamela Sykes provided a few more winners for me before a broken femur brought my season to a close. Winning the Stayers' Hurdle was certainly the cream of a stop and start season. The weather had played its part, I had had a couple of small injuries and as usual a number of days off with concussion, but signs were evident that all was not good with Mercy and this was a concern to me.

After a good holiday, once more fishing in Ireland, I was ready to start again. I was going to stay with Mercy; there was after all both Gaye Chance and Western Rose to look forward to. The latter might be feeling his age a bit and the handicapper had a tight hold of him, but the former must now be a Gold Cup candidate. The season started slowly with very few rides in the West Country, but once the Midlands courses got going in September I had winners for Mercy, which included a double at Hereford, one for her and one for Pamela Sykes. It was soon all go again. Western Rose won at Kempton having been beaten again at Cheltenham. Gaye Chance was third in the Hennessy, although for some unknown reason I was very handy on him and I'm not sure why those were my instructions on this occasion, but doubles followed at Wolverhampton and Wincanton. Back to the old routine and I was enjoying it, most of the time.

I was now well established among the group of senior jockeys riding every day for a number of the leading trainers. My movement up the pecking order in the jockeys' changing rooms had been steady. The changing rooms in the south were divided into two sections: there were two valet teams, one being Johnny Buckingham and his brother Tom, and the other being Robin Lord. We automatically fell into two groups and although I had three good mates in the other team, namely Paul 'Henry Kissenger' Barton – now the senior British Horseracing Authority Stewards Secretary, Colin 'Desert Orchid' Brown and Richard 'Half Free' Linley – now the Senior British Horseracing Authority Course Inspector. My main mates were the guys I sat with day in day out. Smith Eccles, Hywel Davies, Scu and Frank, an elite band, and I was fortunate to be clinging to their coat-tails.

There were ten or twelve of us who travelled the roads of the south of England most days of the week. I hitched a lift as often as I could, particularly down to the West Country meetings, not just because I had long pockets but I always got so tired and had a real danger of falling asleep at the wheel on the way home. John 'Burnt Oak' Suthern, one of David 'the Duke' Nicholson's jockeys, had good wheels at the time and was good to provide both a seat and plenty of entertainment. We knew each other's characters pretty well, and they used to laugh at me as I was always the quickest to get dressed after racing. They said it only took me one movement to put on all my clothes – three or four would be more accurate – but it did not take me long, as almost everything went on at once. It was most frustrating if someone had messed about with my pile, as I always liked to beat the worst of the traffic jams out of the racecourses if I could.

Hywel used to amuse us all, one knee crossed over the other, rolling a cigarette and trying to put the smallest piece of tobacco into it, so it looked like a very small bent twig when he had finally finished his rolling, invariably telling us some amusing tale about Captain Forster, his boss. Frank and Eck would very likely be comparing notes on last night's entertainment or planning the next; they were never short of a good story. Scu was the more serious one, which is probably why he was so damned good, as nothing was left to chance. On the other side of the fence Colin would tell us amusing stories about David Elsworth's latest antics while Paul's imitations of his boss Gandy – David Gandolfo – led Frank to better these impersonations, regularly having us all in stitches.

Frank was brilliantly casual about the whole thing, but he had huge talent and at the time 'the greatest' was not an unreasonable accolade. We played numerous practical jokes on each other. After only a few years of riding I had lost a few front teeth and used to keep my dentures in a soap box when I was riding. One day at Doncaster, Eck rummaged in my racing bag while I was riding in a race which he wasn't and found my soap box, so he went off to the tea room, found a sandwich and placed my dentures into the sandwich placing the combination in the soap box back in my bag. They all enjoyed the shock I got when after racing I opened my soap box and I found my teeth already having that sandwich I had been looking forward to. Steve Smith Eccles – Eck – and I often sat beside each other in the changing room, although he would be quick to point out that he was always above me, and quite rightly so.

Frank was possibly the worst prankster. On one occasion he put the yellow disinfectant lumps from the gents' pee tray onto a plate and pretended to be chewing a large lemon gobstopper. He went through to the weighing room and offered one to the Clerk of the Scales – I don't think he took one! We all had various ways of getting past the scales at the right weight so that our owners thought we had managed not to carry any overweight. Girths were left off, stirrups left off, saddles even passed out of the window, having just weighed out without a saddle at all – not something I was brave enough to do. I did try threading a coat hanger up the long cord of my cap and by placing my cap on my knee as I weighed out, my cord would hang down straight and with the wire in it, I could just put enough weight on it to lift myself up so registering one or two pounds less on the scales. When I stood up I had to be careful not to poke the eye out of the poor official with my straight wire.

The things we tried to do to make life easier for ourselves amused us but would not have amused the officials;

however, getting round them caused us a lot of laughs. Practical jokes were a regular part of the day's entertainment, but sometimes a more serious call on our friendship was required. On a fairly dreary afternoon at Taunton, Frank had a bad fall in the first race and he came back into the changing room looking as white as a ghost and complaining that he thought he had torn his knee ligaments. He went off to the loo muttering that he was going to be sick and he was not ready to see the doctor yet, something we all had to do if we had a fall and were due to ride again that day. Soon after he had limped away the course doctor arrived at the changing room door. 'Mr Francome, where are you?' he requested. More out of devilment than malicious intent, confident he would know the champion jockey, I shouted from the other end of the room, 'Here Sir,' and much to my amazement the good doctor came walking straight up to me and asked me how my knee was. I was too far down the road now to admit he had the wrong man, so I put out my left leg and flexed it up and down. He gave my knee a few prods and told me with a broad smile that I was indeed OK and fit to ride. Frank came back from the loo, still as white as a sheet and limping badly. He thanked me, got himself together and went out to win the last.

We all pushed the limits riding with injuries, covering them up as best we could. I limped out to the parade ring at Uttoxeter one day with my fibula seemingly broken in my left leg and rode at Cheltenham with a broken collarbone, all for the sake of not missing a ride and a possible winner. We would try and help each other if we knew

147

one of us was in pain, going to post and in the early part of the race, but once at the business end any sympathy was out of the window. We talked to each other quite a lot during races, although some of the guys were keener for a chat than others. Eck was always a good one to pass the time with but you could not trust him. One afternoon at Nottingham he shouted over to me saying, 'Kick on Sam, you will win this,' but thankfully I did not take his advice for his intention was for me to hit the front too soon and he was going to come late and beat me. I waited and he was unable to run me out of it at the end. I did try and get the Princess Royal to speak to me going down the back at Ludlow one afternoon; after all, you don't very often get a chance of a one to one with royalty: 'Madam, how are you going?' There was no reply so after we had jumped another fence and she was still beside me I thought perhaps I had got the title wrong and tried 'Ma'am, how are you going?' Still no reply, but things were beginning to get serious so I gave up. To give her her due, on pulling up she was quick to congratulate me on winning and she apologised for not being able to speak. She was at least relaxed enough to hear me!

It was not always fun and games and on occasions someone pushed the boundaries of competitive racing a bit too far. We all tightened each other up a bit closing a gap and not letting someone through. I did just that to a royal runner at Newbury one day and, to avoid a diplomatic incident – I was Irish after all and it was not long after the dreadful Birmingham bombings – an exchange of letters took place. If any interference was thought to be dangerous the culprit would be given more than a slight talking-to back in the changing room. Having had a bad fright, bordering on the dangerous, emotions could run high. There were a few girls riding against us in those days and any quiet private talking-to in the changing room was not possible as they had their own changing room, often in those days very small. On one occasion at Hereford an attractive young lady, now the wife of a very successful Lambourn trainer, went up my inside when as far as I was concerned that was my territory and she was going somewhere she shouldn't. Her tight left buttock got a gentle smack as punishment as I quietly said no to her – the squeal made it worthwhile.

On another occasion, also at Hereford, I had dropped my whip going past the stands and I knew I was going to need mine in a circuit's time, as I was on one of Mercy's that had to win. There was a girl in the race, and she was surely the easiest target. I manoeuvred myself beside her and calmly tried to snatch her whip from her. 'You won't be needing this,' I told her. But much to my annoyance and surprise I was not quick enough and she would not let go, so I had to give up the tug-of-war as there was a hurdle coming up. I did need a whip and we got beaten.

Later in my career I felt the need to react one afternoon at Newton Abbot. I was told that an unusually tall young jockey was telling trainers that I had lost my nerve. Rumours like this could have a serious impact on my career and as I hardly had a nerve in my body, I was even more annoyed. So I went across to this beanpole and asked him what he was up to. He began to get to his feet to defend himself, but before he could tower over me, while informing him quietly that I would have more nerve than he will ever be able to find, I smacked him on the nose. He sat down again.

We were never short of entertainment and one winter's day at Chepstow the fog was so thick we were sure that racing was going to be abandoned. In customary fashion we got weighed out for the next race before the meeting was called off due to the fog as this always ensured we got paid for at least one ride if the meeting was indeed abandonned. The next was a novice chase so we were not particularly keen to go anyway. We were almost at the stage of taking off our boots when the call came to get our helmets on and get going; we were astonished and slightly amused at this decision. When we arrived at the start, five hundred yards down the course from the winning post, the situation was no better. We could hardly see the first fence which was going to be the last after only one circuit in this two-mile contest and we could not see the winning post. We appealed to the starter that this was daft as we could not see where we were going. He said, 'Rubbish,' and called us in and set us off. We jumped the first fence, galloped past the stands and down into the dip and up the other side, but entering the back straight the fog was just as thick if not thicker. As we approached the first fence in the back straight a call came out from one of the boys in front: 'Come on boys, we won't jump this, they can't see us!' It was the time before all racing was televised and they could certainly not see anything from the grandstands, so without thinking any further we all pulled out in a wave. The funniest thing was the reaction of the poor fence men, always doing such a good job repairing the fences and hurdles each time we jump them. These poor guys were startled as we all calmly galloped by not far from where they were standing. Looking back they all must have thought that we had been told to miss out their fence as they never reported anything back to the stewards or the Clerk of the Course. We galloped right down the back straight not jumping a single fence, and turning into the home straight, when the race proper was beginning to develop, I thought we were bound to pull in and jump all the fences in the home straight at least and I suggested we should. 'Rubbish,' was the answer and we carried on missing them out. It was not until the second last that we pulled in and jumped that and then the last fence and one of us went on to win. Nothing was said, the result stood and it remains in the record books as a perfectly normal novice steeplechase at Chepstow!

There were many moments when things were far more serious and the next for me was when Gaye Chance ran badly and only finished fourth at Newbury. This horse was wonderful in so many ways for my career, but he also caused so much tension in my life. It was about this time that we lost Very Promising to David Nicholson's yard and Mercy was fuming. Although I got beaten on all of Mercy's at the two-day Wolverhampton meeting after Christmas, I had three winners over the two days and then had another double before the New Year. Then disaster struck as Gaye Chance broke a hind leg on the gallops. He had been a fantastic friend to us all and this was a crushing blow. Dreams of the Gold Cup were gone forever.

A lot of meetings were lost in February due to snow, Cheltenham came and went with little excitement for me and I went at the first in the National, albeit on a tearaway 100/1 shot. I was happy to ride anything in that race. Thankfully I had some winners for Mercy in May but I was glad to see the end of that season. Annabelle had already gone north to her sheep with my sons Charlie and Harry and I headed across the world to Australia as a member of a jump jockeys' team to represent the UK against the Australians. We behaved as British jump jockeys should on a foreign holiday and made the most of some fantastic Australian hospitality. We had a ball but lost the series. I did win a race on a horse of Nicky Henderson's at Warwick during the return match that autumn which did something to make up for no winners down under.

The 85/86 season started slowly. I had little action down the West Country but the first Worcester meeting got me started with a nice chase winner for Peter Bailey and then I had one for Ginger McCain at Bangor. Pamela had her string in great early form and we had three winners in October. My trainers were coming up trumps and I was nearly in double figures by the middle of October. Then we had a slight problem. Mercy planned to run a smart little horse at Chepstow in what looked like a reasonably competitive handicap hurdle. However, much to my dismay, when I got to the racecourse I was told that the Irish owners wanted me to finish midfield and on no account was I 'to show her up'. Some task this was going to be I thought.

I was undecided about the best course of action. I could just try and ride an appalling race, jump off slowly giving the others a good start and make some late headway, but this might be too obvious I thought. Better perhaps to go off in front very fast, assuming that she will tire and the others would then come by. That was probably the brave and best option but I was worried that she just might stay out in front and then she really would be exposed. I opted for the easiest option, to sit in the middle of the pack and let them go when they quickened, pretending to use my whip if necessary. I sat sixth or seventh and as luck would have it she jumped beautifully and travelled with ease.

Turning into the straight with four flights still to jump, I was travelling as well, if not better, than anyone. No great problem yet as there is a long way to go, I thought. Going to three out it was apparent that nothing was going better than me and much to my horror I could see nothing was going to quicken. I shouted to the boys around me, 'For God's sake lads get going, I'm not fancied!' It must have been music to their ears but they had not got the horse under them to do anything about it. I was sitting as still as a mouse with a slight hold on my left rein, out of sight of the stewards, keeping the little horse in check. Four of my mates were pushing and slapping but still not going away from me and the others had fallen away. Four strides out from the last hurdle the tight little group of four opened up and I knew that sitting still was no longer an option, otherwise I would definitely be called in front of the stewards for not trying.

The best option then would have been to pull up, get off and tell everyone I thought that my mount had gone lame. I am sure this had been done before but in the heat of battle, and it not being something I had ever done before, it was no surprise that I did not think of it. Instead I did the only thing that I thought I could; I let the little horse go, saw a nice stride at the last hurdle and jumped it well, if a fraction right-handed. As I went through the gap there was the slightest contact with the horse on my right ridden by Simon Sherwood, but now the chips were down and we went away to win with a bit in hand. Too bad I thought, but this horse was better than we thought and I had been asked to do the impossible. At least I had a winner under my belt and my explanation to the owners and Mercy would be simple; their precious horse was too good not to win this poor race.

Then I heard the dreaded call over the tannoy of a stewards' enquiry. That was going to be something to look forward to, I thought. Simon and I went into the stewards' room with the expectations that the result would not change, but Simon saw the chance of being promoted and winning was what we were all there for, most of the time. We were asked to watch the head-on film and it was evident that I had jumped very slightly to the right and we had indeed touched, but it was also evident that I had won with something in hand. However, Simon had the gift of the gab and told a good story; there was contact and he argued that had caused interference and stopped him from winning. I should have told them how well I was going just before the last hurdle. The rules as they stood then were on his side. We were sent out while the three stewards made their decision and after what seemed an age we got asked to return to their den. 'We believe that there was interference and it affected the result,'... my heart fell into my boots, and I did not hear any more. Things could not have been much worse; not only had I fully exposed the horse but the consolation of winning the race and at least gaining some prize money had been taken away by the stewards and we had been placed second. However, I should not have been asked to do the impossible and nobody could surely blame me; in fact I expected some sympathy.

This Saturday mishap was not mentioned when riding out again on Monday morning and the business of trying to ride winners carried on relentlessly. I was busy with plenty of rides and the vast majority had some sort of chance three out and fortunately a reasonable percentage entered the winner's enclosure. I was then presented with a definite winner at Newbury. The horse that I had been demoted on at Chepstow, fresh and well after the easy 'win', was very fortunate that, due to the firm ground at Newbury, we were due to have a walkover in what was a very valuable hurdle race. That will at least make up for my losses at Chepstow three weeks earlier I thought. Then Mercy dropped the bombshell that I was not going to ride it. Despite being asked to do the impossible in its previous run and winning on the horse twice before I was being jocked off when all I had to do was ride past the post to collect the winnings. I was dumbstruck and my relationship with my main trainer hit a new low and it never really recovered.

The majority of the owners in the yard still wanted my services and soon we were back on the winning trail with a treble at Warwick, Run And Skip for John Spearing being the highlight in between two for Mercy. Run And Skip was a tough little horse who liked to make the running over three miles or further, although he was prone to the odd mistake, but we got on well and I loved riding him. On to Wolverhampton and another double, one for Pamela and one for Mercy which was followed by a heavy fall in the novice chase. As was often the case, I escaped examination by the first aid boys at the fence and, as it was my last ride of the day, I slipped off home having told the doctor that I was fine. I had been here many times before, feeling slightly sick with a mild headache, but above all else just feeling dull and perhaps slightly sick.

I rang Mercy in the morning, but having had a winner for her the day before that was easier than some mornings. I told her that unfortunately I had concussion and not only would I not be riding out as usual but I should not ride for a few days. I sat out Tuesday getting depressed, as I was missing rides at Leicester, on Wednesday I was a little better but still not good. Pamela had Masterplan in a handicap hurdle at Warwick on Thursday and she wanted to run him. He was a nice easy ride and he had a good chance, or I told myself that anyway. I was not going to sit by and let someone else on him so I persuaded Pamela that I was OK and I would see her at Warwick tomorrow.

I drove to Warwick telling myself that I was fine but knowing I was not 100%. It was only a hurdle race, Masterplan would win and I would feel a whole lot better as a result. With only one ride and that was in the last it was a long day and I was never very good at waiting. As I had escaped the doctor at Wolverhampton, thankfully I did not have to see the course doctor before I rode. Pamela was as usual concerned about my health. She was suspicious and must have asked me ten times whether I was really all right, but I was not going to give in at this late stage. Cantering to post it felt good to be back in the saddle, Masterplan felt great and I was looking forward to getting into battle once again.

I jumped out handy as was my pattern and then took a pull to settle in about sixth place in my usual position on the inside. He felt strong and well, but was if anything a little free and I was having trouble getting him to drop the bit and settle. Just after passing the stands and going up the Warwick hill, two conditional jockeys in front of me started to lose their positions as their mounts bounced off each other, and one of them started to come back towards me due to this squeezing. On a normal day I would have roared at them to keep straight and behave themselves, but instead I just allowed one to drop back onto me. It was an accident waiting to happen but in my slightly dazed mood I did nothing about it. Masterplan clipped the heels of the horse forced to drop back in front of me and down we went like a shot rabbit. As the ten or twelve follow-ing horses clattered over the top of me, forty-three hooves probably missed me but one caught my head a glancing blow, which was exactly what I did not need.

I got to my feet and was brought back to the weighing room in the ambulance; how many times had I done that before. I was asked the now familiar questions of: 'Where are you?' 'What day of the week is it?' 'Who won last season's Gold Cup?' I had been asked that one before in a similar situation, so that one came to mind quite quickly, but the others proved more difficult and another dreaded 'red entry' went into my medical book. I rang Mercy when I got home and told her I had had another fall but that I was fine and would only be off for seven or eight days as that was the time required for a red entry for concussion. Little did I know I was not going to be fit to ride again that season. If I had known that at the time I would have been near suicidal.

I was used to feeling sick for a few days with a mild headache so this was nothing new, but after three weeks with no sign of improvement I was getting not only frus-trated but concerned. Having Christmas at home began to look like a real possibility which had its merits and I would be able to enjoy Christmas with my small family. However, that cloud of concussion was not moving at all and I was missing a lot of rides and had the usual concern that I was not going to get these rides back. I also had a family to feed and I was the only breadwinner.

The Injured Jockeys Fund are there to help jockeys when they are unable to ride due to injury, and I was now to find out what a wonderful job they do. I had a visit from the Almoner in the region who, finding me in a pretty poor state, was just the pick-me-up I needed. There was reassurance that my finances would be secure for as long as I was off work and there was going to be financial assistance for any medical treatment I might need. The warmth and care I felt from that first meeting is something I will never forget.

Unfortunately, despite this reassurance that I had support and could ask for more help, that did not improve my condition. Three weeks of headaches turned into six weeks, Christmas came and went and I began to question whether I would make the Festival. Could this really be happening to me? My career was certainly in tatters. I looked at the results in the morning papers every day as my fortunate friends won on my horses on a hopelessly regular basis. I was not easy to live with. Annabelle tried to make out that losing all these winners did not matter, but I was having nothing of that. I felt helpless and there was no sign of improvement.

We spent some time in Northumberland where, as always, Annabelle's sheep needed some care and attention, but that did nothing to cure my depression. Things did not improve in time for the Festival and I could not even watch as my Run And Skip finished fourth in the Gold Cup. Aintree passed me by as well. The season drew to a close and I was still watching from the sidelines with a headache and feeling sick nearly six months after my fall. It was early May when it was suggested to me that I should try a cranium osteopath in Harley

Street who had cured long-term concussion in the past. I consulted the Injured Jockeys Fund and they agreed to pay for this consultation, so I set off on the first of many trips to London on the train from Gloucester. Black gloss door, brass plates, big brass electric bell, nervously I pressed the button into a daunting new world. Greeted by a white-coated receptionist and ushered into an immaculate but austere waiting room, what was I letting myself into? I did not have to wait long before I was invited to sit in a leather armchair in an immaculate office with the friendly smile of my elderly osteopath, another white coat giving this weird situation even more significance.

I was invited to give some history of my problem, but this did not appear to give any concern. I, however, had huge concern and, having had an X-ray, it was explained to me that I had a compressed fracture of my cranium and this ageing white-haired gentleman was going to manoeuvre my cranium bones back into place and to do this he had to first pull my hair very, very hard to allow him then to move my cranium bones. I was desperate to feel better and to be allowed to ride again; it was just as well I was, as he then proceeded to pull my hair as hard as he possibly could. It did make my eyes water but somehow the level of pain could be coped with and once he finished he started to try and move my cranium bones by placing both his hands on my head and pushing in various directions; it was a strange experience.

After treatment that lasted half an hour I was asked whether I felt any better to which, after this first treatment, the answer was no. I was asked to come back for more in two weeks. It took a bit of courage to get back on that train two weeks later but I did. This time, much to my relief, halfway through the treatment I felt my sickness lift and I definitely felt a real clarity in my awareness – what a great feeling that was. I was asked to walk round the Harley Street block and remember which house number I got to before my concussion came back. Unfortunately I only got about twenty doors down. However, this had to be seen as progress and my consultant was pleased. I continued to take that train to London every two weeks for two months, until I could very nearly walk right round the Harley Street block without the dreaded gloom returning again.

However, after fourteen weeks and seven treatments I decided that I had had enough and I began to think this guy had control of me. He could certainly make me a bit better but I was concerned he could also make me worse. I said my thanks and said goodbye to Harley Street on this occasion. I had certainly gone through a lot of pain and a lot of travelling and the Injured Jockeys Fund had gone through considerable expense. I will never know if it was all worthwhile but thankfully after three quiet weeks at our home in Birtsmorton the awful cloud of concussion began to lift and I felt able to ride out again.

I had though lost my place in more ways than one. I had probably lost my main source of income, the Kinnersley string. Mercy had always showed concern about my injury but our relationship was getting worse and while I was enjoying riding her horses I always rather stupidly felt under pressure as I did not think she wanted me on them. I was only on board because the owners wanted me and some of her owners did remain wonderfully loyal. Pamela Sykes had a nice string of about eight and she did not want anyone else to ride them and I was also soon riding out regularly for John Spearing and Peter Bailey. While things were not desperate, the future was going to be tough, although I felt better which was a huge relief, and I was soon to be back on the racetrack doing what I loved. It certainly never crossed my mind that owners and trainers might be cautious about putting me up knowing I was damaged goods and a fall on one of their horses would possibly cause me long-term injury again, or worse.

I was now desperate to get back on the racecourse, prove to myself that I had fully recovered and to prove to others that I was able to continue my career. I needed to feel the wind in my face, to hear the crash of birch around me and be among my mates in the changing room. There was some media interest when, after nine months off with a head injury, I announced that I would ride again at the start of the season. Interest increased when the scribes got the news that my first ride back looked like being in a novice chase. Karnatak had jumped well over John Spearing's small schooling fences – some way off the best schooling facilities I had come across – but they served their purpose and it did not take long before John and I knew that Karnatak had a good jump in him and would also be keen to look after himself, which importantly meant he would also be looking after me. Despite the concern others were showing, I knew that this was an ideal opportunity for me to restart my career.

As always at the start of the season the changing room was a buzz of activity: stories of the summer holidays, who had got hitched to whom, who had broken up with whom, new wives, new babies and new jobs and I had been away from all this for a while, so there was plenty to catch up on. I needed to find out who was riding for whom this season and which of the yards looked like being the dominant players as the season progressed since this was vital information that I needed to absorb in my new role as a freelance jockey. I had a good string of trainers who appeared keen to put me up, but I knew without the Kinnersley big guns to keep my name in the papers – although Gaye Chance had gone and Western Rose had been retired – I was going to have to look for new opportunities.

Newton Abbot had been good to me over the years and this second day of August 1986 was no exception. As I grabbed my whip and helmet, my mates in the changing rooms wished me well. I got a leg up on Karnatak and walked around the parade ring; a lot of punters were also aware of this big moment for me and wished me luck as well. On this occasion I just needed not to be unlucky and I wasn't. Karnatak proved to be a good bit better than his rivals. He jumped impeccably, we led two out and he won easily. It was great to be back and to come back with a winner was quite special, with the Newton Abbot crowd giving me a warm welcome back to the winner's enclosure. My head felt good. I was fully aware

of all around me and I was definitely back in the starting blocks. Annabelle was pleased when I got home and
hoped we could now look forward to more of the same.
I knew that it was going to be a tough road ahead, but
I could not have got off to a better start. A week later
Karnatak won at Worcester and again at Hereford, three
times in as many weeks, which was just what I needed.
I had a winner for Richard Barber at Wincanton and
one for Peter Bailey at Worcester. Things could not have
started much better.

As the season properly got underway I began to feel
that, if I was not careful, the big meetings would pass me
by. Mercy had a winner locally ridden by John Bryan,
who now appeared to be flavour of the month, but then
Pamela came to the rescue, bravely sending Itsgottabeal-
right all the way from her yard in the Welsh Borders to
Kempton, where we won a fast and furious two-mile
chase. If ever a horse liked to stand back and jump it
was him, so needless to say we got on well. I had a ride
for Mercy at that meeting, and I thought it ran well but
it did not finish in the three, so it was going to take a
lot more than that to get me back in favour. However,
winning both the handicap chase on Rogario for Peter
Bailey and the novice chase on Masterplan for Pamela at
Stratford in the first week of November provided a boost
to my confidence.

The season continued in much the same way. I was
not having quite as many rides as before, but four or
five trainers were using my services on a regular basis,
not on all their horses I may add, but winners were

coming nearly every week. Boxing Day did not provide its usual rewards when I was second on one for Mercy and managed to wrestle to the ground, when challenging two out, my only ride for Fred Winter. Thankfully Peter Bailey still had some nice horses for me to ride despite an awkward unseat at Newbury and we had some fun, and John Roberts came up with the goods with Atataho at Stratford before the end of the year. I had some near misses for Mercy but also some good winners, thank goodness. One was Eton Rouge who I just got past the post in front in a steeplechase at Chepstow the Saturday before Cheltenham, but I needed more than that boost of confidence to do anything with my meagre pickings at the showcase meeting the following week. I did have two spins for Mercy, but that was all they did, get round, but Mercy won the Arkle with Gala's Image which kept her beaming, most of the time. I found myself at Hereford on Grand National day, and the only consolation was that my friend Hywel Davies was there too, but it was not the place for any senior jockey to be on Grand National day. To make matters worse the meeting was abandoned halfway through as the course became waterlogged from very heavy rain all afternoon. From there the season petered out; I had a couple more winners before a fall cut short the season by three weeks for me.

I came back from my summer break as keen as ever. A boot full of frozen salmon had come back from the west of Ireland after a great week on the Owenmore, so any Sunday lunch parties were sorted for a while, but I needed to get fit now and get some early rides booked.

I was determined not to slip further down the scale, but I needed to find some good horses to ride and to start with, some early rides in August were essential. I never enjoyed running to get fit so out came my bicycle. The quiet roads around Birtsmorton were ideal and if I felt like a climb up the Malvern Hills, the challenge was always there. I preferred to ride out for my small trainers and hit the road as often as possible in the remaining three weeks of July before the season opened as usual at Newton Abbot in the first week of August.

My new trainer in the West Country, John Roberts, was keen to make use of my experience and I combined a trip to the races with riding out for him one day. He had a nice little yard stuck away in the hills on the edge of Exmoor. Small fields surrounded by high banks dotted with pretty hamlets, great country. A lot of his horses were not quite in the great category but John had high hopes for some and he was pleased to have my services. This was going to be another string to my bow and I hoped it would be useful to get my season underway providing me with rides at the early West Country meetings.

I had had quite a busy first week of the season riding at four different meetings with one winner under my belt for Peter Bailey at Devon and Exeter; I was looking forward to a good season riding for him at least. I had two rides on the first Saturday at Worcester – little Native Break ran well to finish second in the handicap chase and my second ride was for John in the novice chase. Americk had some hurdle form, but his previous attempts at fences had not been good and he had fallen and thrown his chances away with bad mistakes. John warned me to be careful and a good school round would perhaps be the best approach, although his hurdle form indicated that he was good enough to win this sort of contest. I had already had a second that afternoon and in my mind, as always, I was ready to go one better.

He felt fit and well going to post and he appeared to go well on the very fast ground we had that afternoon. I jumped off mid-division in a field of twelve at the bottom of the home straight. He jumped well up over those first four fences and, keeping a tight hold, I dropped back a bit as we passed the stands, after which he jumped the first down the back well and cleared the water without trouble. My competitive brain then took over. He is jumping well, going better than a lot of those around me, and I think I can pull off a surprise here – that was my thought process. I had ridden a lot of 33/1 winners, so why not this one? I loosened my hold on him and gave him a slap down the shoulder; it was time to get competitive. Going that little bit quicker we met the next fence all wrong. As had been the case so many times in my career I gave him the encouragement to stand back and jump but he did not have the confidence to do that and tried to put another stride in. We hit the fence halfway up and we were into a somersault.

The next thing I knew was that I was in hospital, I was only half-conscious, I could see very little and could not speak. Both a doctor and a nurse were with me and they explained that I was about to go and have an operation on my face as I had a number of bones broken and had lost a

167

lot of teeth with it. I was not aware of anything, although I did take in that I was not to be frightened when I woke up to find I could not open my mouth as my jaws were going to be wired together and to start with I would have difficulty breathing. I was assured that when I did wake there would be someone with me. I would, they assured me, manage okay and get used to it. I was wheeled off on a trolley with a needle hovering. It was indeed scary waking up with the very real fear that I could not breathe and would suffocate as anticipated, but with the help of a sympathetic nurse I found I could breathe, albeit with difficulty at first, so that problem was only a minor one.

Annabelle was her usual calm self when she came and saw me that evening. As my face was like a football and all colours of the rainbow I did suggest that it was perhaps unwise for her to bring my two boys in to see me just yet, although I was dying to give them each a big hug and tell them that their Dad was better than he looked. I enjoyed a number of visits from my mates from the weighing room and some of the Worcester racecourse officials were kind enough to pay me a visit. Perhaps they knew more about my future than I did, or perhaps they were relieved they did not have a fatality on their hands. I was going to be all right, despite a reported seven broken bones in my face and the necessity to remove seven crushed teeth. I had hit the very firm ground, face first. I was wired up with a mixture of wire and elastic bands and these had to stay in place for eight weeks. I was allowed home after a week and my recuperation took place in much more pleasant surroundings.

To take my mind off racing and yet more rides I was missing and would miss with this long layoff, I thought a fishing trip was a good idea and looking back I have no idea why the Outer Hebrides beckoned and the lochs of South Uist. One of my best fishing companions had always been my cousin Angus and he was game for the trip. I met him off the train at Oban and we set off on the quite substantial sea crossing to South Uist. One thing I was advised is that I must have a pair of scissors handy if I was going to vomit otherwise I was in danger of drowning. The wind was blowing a howler and I always got seasick, so this was not looking good. To try and help the situation Angus offered me an apple. 'How on earth can I eat that with my jaw all wired up?' I replied. I cannot recall whether we caught many fish or not but the Lochboisdale Hotel looked after us well and any shortage of fish on the bank certainly would not have been from the lack of trying.

The eight weeks went by without any more excitements, but a large red entry in my little black book told me I was not to consider riding until 1st November and I then needed to be passed by the Senior Jockey Club Medical Officer. I cannot deny that I was sore and that it was going to take a lot for me to start on that road back, but it was my job. I was only thirty-two and I knew I could still earn a respectable living race riding for at least another couple of years. The first day of November arrived and, having made my appointment to see the Jockey Club doctor on the first occasion I could, I set off to London on the train. I was a bit scared as I really did not know what the outcome was going to be or to be honest what I wanted it to be. The doctor certainly had my future in his hands and he was going to be the sole decision maker.

I had come across Dr Allen quite a lot – there is a cartoon of him looking into my eyes at Newbury with a torch, saying, 'The lights are on but nobody is at home!' I hoped this was not going to influence his decision. I do not remember anything about the interview but I very clearly remember standing on the steps of the London Portman Square offices without a job and simply no idea of what I was going to do in the future. Dr Allen had simply informed me that my head had taken too many bashings and he felt it was unsafe for me to race ride again. My licence to ride was withdrawn forthwith. It was a long and lonely train journey home, and, as it was before the time of mobile phones, it was two and a half hours later before I was able to share this devastating news with my wife and family. The bell had been rung on my riding career.

We both knew that I was a long way from right and I knew that I was not sure whether I could commit myself to it all again, but I kept these thoughts firmly to myself. The swelling was long gone but an appointment to see my surgeon again was looming. My nose had obviously taken a bashing. I remember after my operation he said with some amusement that he had been able to improve it from the effects of other falls but the airways were not quite as good as they might be and could give me problems in the future. Clearing them was an interesting experience as two rubber tubes were inserted up either nostril, harmless enough, until he expanded them with jets of air. The effect was very painful but it seemed to ensure the desired improvement and I could breathe freely again. The pain of this and the very intense memory of the facial fractures I had encountered was not something I wanted to go through again. I found that while the pain from other breaks and bruises could somehow be pushed away and kept at bay, pain in my face was literally 'in my face' and was impossible to keep at arm's length.

I had ridden over four hundred winners, had a lot of fun and I thought I was now ready to walk away from it, thankfully in one piece, or just about. However, I had no idea where the next pay cheque was going to come from. Fortunately, I was provided with a lifesaving cushion by the Injured Jockeys Fund. Having paid, like every other professional jockey, a very small amount from every ride into a compensation fund, I was now going to get back all of that with interest for twelve months, and what a help that was.

My Working Life

I WASN'T SURE which route to take. I had kept a clean sheet in my riding days, well as clean as anyone could in those days, and a job working for the Jockey Club seemed the obvious route to take. In early November an advertisement for a Stewards' Secretary appeared in the *Sporting Life* and I got the nod that if I applied I would have a good chance to be the first ex-professional jockey to be employed in this important role, a route the Jockey Club wanted to explore for the first time. Although this was a huge compliment, I was only partially tempted as all the travelling involved was not attractive to me. I also thought that role was a bit serious for me and I would not be able to behave well enough all the time. However, I put my name in the hat and was soon informed that I was to be one of three interviewed for the post. Almost the following day an advert appeared in the *Sporting Life* for an Assistant Clerk of the Course at Ayr Racecourse. I had met a lot of Clerks and got to know some of them quite well. You could not meet a nicer man than Hugo Bevan, Clerk of the Course at Towcester and Huntingdon, and if he was a typical example there must be some fun in the job. I applied and was soon on my way up to Ayr for an interview. I never did sit the Jockey Club interview.

As with so many things in my life, I was in the right place at the right time. The first money was beginning to flow to the racecourses from the sale of their racing pictures live into the betting shops, live pictures rather than the previous audio only feed, and they felt flush with money. They liked what Morag Gray, the only other interviewee, had to offer and remarkably they thought they could do something with me, so they took us both on. Morag had a lot more business skills than I had, although that would not have been difficult. I famously offered to go to night school to learn more, but that offer was declined, thank goodness.

Colonel Greig was the Chairman, a wonderfully kind man, and his executive team was led by Colonel Bill McHarg and his son David. Bill McHarg took me under his wing; he was a man of immense integrity, a wealth of knowledge and a nice sense of humour. For the first week or two I did my best to listen and to look busy, if nothing else. This was certainly new territory, as I had never in my wildest dreams seen myself working all day behind a desk, but this is what life was going to be like from now on and I had better get used to it.

My digs at this time consisted, for the first six weeks, of a tiny room in the back of a small hotel on the south side of Ayr. My family had moved up to Annabelle's home estate in Northumberland and Annabelle told me that any move up to Ayr was not something she wanted to consider. Like so many of my friends, the change in the way of life once a jockey's life comes to an end puts a huge strain on a marriage and sadly ours fell apart. Annabelle and I were very fortunate to cash in on the property boom of the mid-eighties and sell our nice house at Birtsmorton for what seemed like a fortune to me, thanks partially to me turning our falling down outbuildings into useful buildings in their own right; I enjoyed a bit of brickwork. Morton House became Morton House Estate and all of a sudden we had three houses to sell. The money raised was soon to be swallowed up in the very expensive education Annabelle now planned for our two boys, but it was a great hit.

A special person came into my life and, for a while, we had a pretty idyllic life in Ayrshire, although not seeing enough of my boys hit me hard and she had to be away a lot. I was lonely at times and I found, much to my dismay, that I was still suffering from the bashes on the head that I had had over the years. Any jolt up my spine, even sitting down too firmly onto a hard chair could trigger a headache and concentrating for more than two hours at my desk brought them back, or at least that was what I put it down to. This meant that I spent more time walking the course at Ayr than perhaps was expected of me, but any time spent with the head groundsman, Bob Dempsey, was time well spent indeed. I was in the hands of not only an expert in his chosen field but also a perfectionist and he knew not only every blade of grass and every yard of drain on Ayr Racecourse but he also knew every screw and nail in the grandstands. Needless to say, his staff loved him.

At that time the management team at Ayr were contracted out to run and provide the Clerk at the other four racecourses in Scotland, so under the guidance of Bill McHarg's son David, I was soon able to get experience of all five. The two other jumping tracks, Kelso and Perth, I knew from my riding days. I had won on Good Prospect at Perth, unfortunately beating Lucius owned, unbeknown to me at the time, by the future chairman of Perth and now my good friend David Whitaker and his wife Fiona. Edinburgh, as it was then called, had just become dual purpose and David McHarg had had the foresight that the sandy soil by the sea would provide the ideal surface for a winter jumps track. Hamilton Park, situated on the southern outskirts of Glasgow, had also been a pioneer, being the first course in the United Kingdom to hold an evening meeting. I was fortunate to be joining a good team.

It was not long before I had one of the first mobile phones, a brick of considerable size. I thought I was the bee's knees and could manage this sort of thing. I am sure it was a coincidence but it was not long after this that I was back unfortunately in concussion mode. A car trying to overtake on the notorious Eaglesham road across the top to East Kilbride, our route to all four of the other racecourses, clipped the car in front and slammed into me knocking me off the road. The impact was enough to shake up my still fragile head and it was bad enough for me to claim some accident insurance compensation, which I got. Concentrating at my desk was even more difficult for a while and headaches were back with a vengeance.

It was not long before Morag and I were sent round to other racecourses as part of our official Clerks' training. I was lucky to spend a day with Richard Osgood at Newbury, one of the most respected head groundsmen in the business. Not sure what he made of me but I did my best to take it all in. Among other things we walked the course prodding our sticks in every few yards. I was certainly soon to learn that the description of the going was to become the most contentious detail in my new working life as a Clerk of the Course, or to put it correctly my first job, as riding horses to me had never been a job, it was simply getting at times well paid for doing something I enjoyed.

I was soon to learn that every Tom, Dick and Harry had their opinion on the going and for some reason that I was never to grasp, a number of people seemed to have the opinion that the description Clerks gave was invariably done for their personal benefit. What could possibly be their personal benefit when to get the going wrong was not only a great inconvenience to owners and trainers but, in doing so, caused us a whole lot of grief? There were to be occasions in the years ahead that it simply had to be spelt out in plain words that, since the last going report was given, if the sun shines the ground dries out and if it rains the ground gets softer; that was not rocket science. Going reports are subjective; mistakes were made I am sure, but we didn't half pay for it.

I was given my first official Clerking day at Perth in August 1988. Jill Grant was the Racecourse Secretary and, looking over the top of her glasses at me, invariably in some amazement, seemed to do just about everything.

Donald Gow was the groundsman and as far as I could see, and I was happy to believe, had knowledge and skills beyond his years. The stewards arrived two hours before racing and their main focus seemed to be the quality of their lunch and how good the port was. It was so stupid of me to be frightened of these good folk when I was riding. My first two days at Perth went without drama and I enjoyed it. The final two days of the short Perth programme in the third week of September went without a hitch as well. David McHarg told me that he would now step away from Perth and the 1989 season was all mine to work with, including the first three-day meeting the course had ever had in April 1989.

I knew we had to do something special with these three days' racing on the bounce, so it concentrated my mind for a few weeks. I could see that there was an opportunity to divert some quality horses from the big Scottish Grand National meeting at Ayr which was going to be the weekend immediately before our midweek three days. Having Clerked at Ayr I knew what races worked there which I could not compete with, I also knew the gaps. I also knew that the ground invariably dried out for this prestigious fixture and, being further north and a different ground composition, Perth had a good chance of having softer and therefore safer ground than Ayr. We were also a very different type of track and, with the new money coming from the sale of our picture rights, we could compete on prize money. I also knew that the trainers and jockeys were ready to let their hair down after a long and stressful season, and they should be ready to party.

The Perth Festival was born and what a party we had. Trainers came, including my good friends Kim Bailey and Nigel Twiston-Davies – both with considerable fire-power – jockeys and stable staff enjoyed themselves, more horses came and sponsors followed. A carnival was born. The racing by day was more competitive than the course had ever had before and the festival mood rolled into town for late night jockeys' quiz parties, karaoke and live music, all of which I had to host; we all had a ball. Working the following day was not easy but I was carried along by the euphoria of it all and thankfully I have never been one to drink. The first festival was the catalyst for twenty years of growth.

Over the next two or three years I Clerked at all five Scottish courses. The responsibility of the Western Meeting and the Scottish National meeting at Ayr was awesome and for a while it was mostly fun. The continued experience of putting on race meetings week in week out did allow me to see every side of the testing lives trainers have. The wrath and remarkable language of one trainer down the phone when I had to tell him his horses would have to stay overnight at Hamilton the night before the Western Meeting at Ayr because all 171 stables at Ayr were full will never be forgotten.

Clerking is a thankless 24/7 job, and I was only enjoying some of the days and had no control of my destiny or, more importantly, the racecourses where I was working. It appeared to me that now was the right time for Perth to break away from Ayr and stand on its own feet. I suggested this to the Chairman at the time, Ronnie Thorburn, and thankfully he agreed. It was plain to me that Perth could not only manage on its own but would be much better for it. Being linked as it was to Ayr was fine if Perth just wanted to open its gates for the meagre fixture list it had and survive on Levy Board subsidy, but its long-term future would unquestionably have been in doubt. To survive in the increasingly competitive world we were moving into, it had to stand on its own two feet. I saw it had huge potential and, although I was far from sure I had the brains to take it on, I knew I had the energy and enthusiasm.

There were to be many new challenges ahead. My job and certainly my enjoyment at Ayr was not looking good. There had been a lot of grief at Ayr and, while we were on an upward curve and attendance was growing again, we needed a new full-time manager and I suggested to the chairman at the time, my friend and colossus of a man Major Ivan Straker, that I knew of a capable person from the south who I thought would be good for the job. I think that was the worst bit of advice I ever gave anybody! Team spirit fell away, smiling faces gone and heads were looking for pennies on the ground rather than tenners in the sky. Despite me providing hospitality and a bed when this fellow first came up to Ayr, it was soon obvious he wanted me out. I was not going to stay around long enough while he made my life miserable. I had a broken leg at the time and things were tough enough anyway, so I made my departure. To make matters worse, while tidying up my farmhouse, I lit a fire to burn the inevitable rubbish and promptly burnt most of the steading down. If it doesn't rain it pours, certainly in my life.

I had broken my leg riding out for Peter Beaumont in Yorkshire. I was down staying with Anthea, daughter of the legendary trainer, who needless to say I had met at one of the Perth Festival parties. I allowed a precious young horse to slip over in the snow on the side of the hill. I lay in the snow and saw my lower leg was at a very funny angle, although strangely enough it was not sore until Peter lifted me up when it was obvious it was just hanging by the skin and was a bad break with both bones snapped in two. Peter drove me straight to York Hospital rather than wait for an ambulance as it was minus something in the wind. Getting out of his Land Rover the paramedic, who had come out to help us, promptly shut my fingers in the Land Rover door!

Things soon improved. The surgeons did a great job, put a long pin down my leg from knee to ankle and everything has been near-perfect ever since. Anthea was one of the best girl jump jockeys of her generation, winning the Topham Trophy over the Grand National fences on J-J-Henry being the highlight, and she was now keen to start training. We were house-hunting in Yorkshire and, if we had found one at this time, things could have been quite different. But the cards did not fall that way and we moved north to be near Perth. We found a nice old house on the banks of the River Earn with our son, Henry. He could nearly ride before he could walk and was to have great fun eventing on some very special ponies. Within a year Anthea was going to take the Clerking role at Perth out of my hands, allowing me to concentrate on the public's requirements on racedays and what a good Clerk she was going to become. She was soon

Clerking at Musselburgh as well, meaning she was unfortunately away from home a lot.

I enjoyed the politics of the industry and I thought I was now getting a pretty good handle on it all. The Jockey Club had run the show for certainly more years than I could remember so not surprisingly, as the commercial world got more and more competitive, there were moves afoot that these well-meaning Gentlemen of the Sport were not up to it. So licensing and integrity were left with them and a new executive team was formed calling itself the British Horseracing Board. They were to deal with the fixtures, the race planning, prize money and a host of other things, and they saw themselves as the driving force behind the industry.

This had all evolved a bit before my time, but the aftermath and indeed some shockwaves were still evident. It was never an easy relationship, not helped when the BHA Chief Executives appeared to come and go like the tide; was that because they faced an impossible task? Then to throw into the mix the Racecourse Association, who are meant to safeguard the interests of all sixty or so racecourses, another impossible task, and you really did have a cocktail for trouble. Meanwhile the Jockey Club, seeing the opportunities that media rights income was creating for the racecourses, began to play a strong hand in the ownership of the largest group of racecourses in the country, including the flagship courses Cheltenham and York.

A new media company calling itself Racing UK had successfully attracted a lot of the big racecourses under their banner – and some of the small ones – to form a powerful media group to be a competitor to the original single operators, Satellite Information Services, in selling our pictures to the bookmakers and into their betting shops. Unfortunately, due to some or indeed most of the bookmakers now trading partially, or in some cases fully, offshore, from where they were not paying betting tax, the levy had fallen considerably and continues to do so.

Yet another group was then formed, conveniently called the Horsemen's Group to try and ensure that a fair share of the money coming into the sport from picture deals was divided largely to the benefit of the owners. What a pig's dinner it was. The income coming into the sport from betting tax has almost halved and this shortfall was not being made up by the increase in income from picture deals, with the result being a worrying decline in the level of prize money available to our owners, without whom there would be no racing industry. Negotiations were never helped by the big racecourses fighting in every way they could find to take the lion's share of any new money coming into the sport. I enjoyed this fight and the argument that many of us used was if the racecourses were put in a pyramid, with Cheltenham, York and Ascot at the top, they would not get the runners they do without a healthy base to the pyramid.

The smaller racecourses had a vital role to play: Newton Abbot, Cartmel and Perth were prime examples. They could attract bigger crowds than many, and often the importance of actually attracting people to go racing has been forgotten. A fun day out at Perth or Cartmel can often lead to aspirations of days out on the bigger stage. The small racecourses also provide the nursery ground for the equine stars of the future. That argument will roll and roll but it would be awfully sad to lose any of the smaller racecourses due to the greed of their bigger neighbours. It was with that fear in mind that, when our media contract came up for renewal a few years later, I proposed to our committee that we should change our media partner from Satellite Information Services and join the more powerful group in Racing UK. I knew we could contribute to this group but we would also be protected by the big players and not threatened by them; the future was more secure.

To me Perth was a jewel just waiting to be polished. It was in the most beautiful setting, with the stunning backdrop of Scone Palace and bordered by the impressive River Tay. More water flows down the Tay than any other river in the UK and from glancing down the river from near the two-mile start at Perth, by the number of salmon seen jumping in the air at one time on one of my first visits to the course, no river in the UK has more salmon running up it. I have been fortunate to have the chance to catch one or two, and some big sea trout, in sight of this beautiful racecourse, but my main focus and time had to be shining and developing this jewel.

My first priority once I arrived on the scene was to improve and invest in the racing surface. We had to get horses to travel past a lot of other racecourses and the opportunities they could offer, so it could not be all about the fun and hospitality when they got to us. We improved the track quite dramatically, we drained and we continually aerated the ground, the sward improved and gradually our turf quality was something we could be proud of; plus we widened it where we could. I have Donald Gow and his best mate Derek Halley to thank for this transformation, as they shared my passion and both had the qualities to be head groundsman at any course in the United Kingdom. They did persuade me to invest in some pretty awesome equipment as well, and it was money well spent.

The Irish were also now travelling over on a regular basis adding sauce to an already exciting cocktail. With more runners, both from the UK and Ireland, we needed a bigger parade ring, and with that came the opportunity to convert the saddling boxes into parade ring hospitality suites. More horses meant more jockeys so we increased the size of the jockeys' changing room and gave them a nice tea room and rest room and, of course, the dreaded sauna. From my own riding days I knew that this would be popular. In a very short time together we had made quite a few changes, enlarging and increasing the facilities; things were beginning to take shape and I was having fun.

With live racing now going into the betting shops the bookmakers needed our product more and more to maximise their profits. They liked to have a race every ten minutes, although in the early nineties this was not possible, so more fixtures were needed. The idea of solving this problem in the summer by not ending the jump season at the end of May and starting again in August and to allow us to race in June and July was aired. Not surprisingly I saw this as a great opportunity for Perth, but what is more, the powers that be – the BHA – were also going to dish out a few Sunday fixtures. Thankfully I was on one of my good days and grabbed the opportunities that would suit us best. We increased our fixture list by four and with that we had two golden Sundays to attract big crowds.

Our first Sunday, themed as Perth Gold Cup day in June 1990, attracted a crowd of 10,000. If Cheltenham had a Gold Cup, why not Perth? I was quite honestly scared about having so many people on the premises, and far too many in the centre of the course were drunk as well, but it was damned exciting. It brought with it problems, and not enough toilets was a regular one. On one occasion, when getting extra mobile toilets in, they had been put in the wrong place and, in my usual way of doing everything myself, I went to move one, pushed it over to one side, only to hear a terrible squeal – there was a young lady already in it!

Our racing had enjoyed a fantastic upward curve in the early nineties and with that sponsorship had increased a hundredfold. I really enjoyed the challenge of attracting new sponsors. To me it was like my favourite sport fly fishing – you cast a lot, you rise quite a few and you land some of those. It was like selling ice cream to children; I knew once they tasted it they would enjoy it and they would come back for more. We had a good product and I enjoyed selling it.

Thankfully some serious players loved what we had created in the festival. Philip Nelson and Guy Morrison, two London-based brokers, came to the party from almost year one and are still coming back today in one form or another and generous sponsorship is still forthcoming. We were also very fortunate that the oil and gas industry in the north-east of Scotland was beginning to take off and the major players in Aberdeen needed somewhere to play and let off steam, as well as do good business; we were expanding at just the right time. Aberdeen Asset Management came on board and supported us, soon followed by the main broadsheet in the region, the *Press and Journal*. We used this partnership to spread the word about the fun that could be had at Perth races to great effect. Coach loads of keen racegoers from Aberdeen soon became the norm giving us a new problem, although a nice one to have – coach parking space. On one notable occasion we had one hundred and one coaches to park; it was indeed boom time for us all.

The next stage was to get our non-raceday income growing and to do that we had to improve our facilities. We needed a new grandstand. My way of going about this was far from conventional but I had got away with it so far and this time I presented plans that my good friend and renowned local architect, Jimmy Denholm, had drawn up. He was renowned for his houses though and this was his first public grandstand, and this was going to cost us in the end. My ever-patient and supportive chairman, David Whitaker, and the committee to whom I was answerable, gave the plans the nod, and we put the plans out to tender.

One of the major construction companies in Scotland got the job. I was naive enough not to know that building contractors of this size are not builders themselves, but they contract everything out and have a far bigger team of lawyers and accountants than they do brickies. What a challenge this was going to be, not helped because I was adamant that we were not going to lose a race meeting during this build, so the whole thing had to be completed between 1st October and 20th April, the first day of our April Festival. It was fraught with problems and near disasters but we got it done, although the construction company were far from our best friends afterwards.

The Right Honourable Alex Salmond officially opened a spacious new grandstand with a fabulous 200-seater viewing restaurant on the first day of our April festival in 2005 – it had cost us £2.2m. What a good investment it turned out to be, as this building was not only going to provide a wonderful modern raceday facility but it was going to transform our non-raceday business. We have now completed the ten-year repayment plan on time with both the Levy Board and the Allied Irish Bank, two great friends to British racing. Philip Nelson agreed with my only partially serious suggestion in 2004 that an invest-ment in bricks and mortar would be a good idea, and his investment got us over the line. With the crash that hit us all in 2008 this was not perhaps such a daft idea after all. Our Nelson Stand is not named after that great admiral of the seas as is sometimes suggested.

Racecourse caterers are of course a crucial part of the operation. They provide the food and the drink and we get some of the profit to reinvest in our facilities or prize money. If only it was as simple as that. To them it is all about driving percentages, so much so that I called our catering manager Mr Percentage Man. We got on well but he used to drive me mad. Any ideas we might have to enhance the day for our customers, the calculator had to come out, number-crunching took place and if the bottom line did not reach the profit percentage he needed he would try and knock it on the head. It was a continual battle which needed to be won to ensure my team did not lose their enthusiasm for new and often exciting ideas. I needed to keep the troops happy and I enjoyed the fight.

Racecourse food is always a contentious issue. We had an annual tasting, which was a bit of a joke really. We needed the likes of Gregg Wallace, of Master Chef fame, to make constructive criticism but we always had a good lunch and ate far too much. The cost of drink at the racecourse was always a nightmare. How could we charge so much when you can get the same bottle of wine in the local supermarket for a tenner or even less. It was Mr Percentage Man again. My emphasis remained that the customer came first and a day out at the races must not be spoilt by excessive prices. We were a sporting venue and costs had to be comparable to other venues, if not better. Catering issues took up a surprising amount of my time. I was never good at percentages; maybe I should have gone to night school after all!

It was about this time that my life took another big turn which was going to be life-changing. I fell in love, it was as simple as that, but unfortunately the consequences were not straightforward, are they ever? I had met Sue briefly a couple of times and knew her well enough to put my arm round her when I found her crying in church one Sunday morning. That moment lifted me high into the sky, a wonderful feeling I was never to lose. We talked on the telephone and sometimes met on the road home from our work in Perth. A mutual friend of ours must have seen us on the roadside and thought it best to tell Anthea. The result was too hard for me to handle and I had to leave home. The idea was to cool off but I could not; perhaps I was weak, but I knew I had found someone very special and someone I wanted to spend the rest of my life with. Sue had left her husband, hence the tears, and we were able to move in together fairly quickly. Some undoubtedly thought too quickly, but the circumstances were such that it fitted for us both and we wanted to be with each other. We married three years later having moved to a house we found together on the edge of Loch Earn in St Fillans. I had finally found peace in my life. We fished together, we watched wildlife together – finding otters was our particular passion. We would walk the west coast looking for them, and on one memorable occasion a mother and her two tiny pups swam by within three yards of the rock we were sitting on and another otter jumped up with his small fish onto the rock beside us. We loved the joys the Scottish countryside offers and we always enjoyed it together in a peaceful, quiet way.

Huge strife was soon to overtake us though when, two years after we found each other, Sue got breast cancer. She fought this with huge stoicism and that remarkable attribute continued when a brain tumour was then diag-

nosed a year later. Over the next four years she was going
to have three brain operations, all the time giving us both
hope, but the end came in June 2015 when she died
peacefully in my arms, only days after her sixtieth birth-
day. We were the same age and could have been born
within five minutes of each other, and we always felt we
were made with the same mixture. She gave me the confidence to be me and I know I have so much to thank
her for; I will, however, never get over her. Her children
Fiona and Andrew are now an inspiration to me.

The bookmakers were still pushing for yet more fixtures and I was able to seize the opportunity to have
our first Saturday fixture. Although we were going to
provide valuable opportunities for the horse popula-
tion and generate valuable levy we had to pay for the
whole fixture ourselves, and that included £60,000 prize
money. The full cost of integrity, which meant the BHA
officials, would, however, be paid for in the usual way
– how generous was that? However, we did have a ball,
and we managed to raise £235,000 for The Prince's
Charity, attracted a crowd of 12,000, including the Duke
and Duchess of Rothesay and made a profit of nearly
£100,000. I guess this has to go down as my single
biggest achievement. It was an awesome day. Apart from
pushing for Perth to take this opportunity, being enthusi-
astic about it and having some ideas how we might make
the day very attractive in order to ensure a big crowd, I
cannot take credit for much else. Alex Salmond, who was
First Minister of Scotland at the time, was the person
who really put the noughts on the figure we managed to

raise. The First Minister was great to work with and we got on well. It was fun to see how politics work at first hand. You scratch my back and I might scratch yours, is the easiest way I can describe it. Big business in Scotland was tapped for sponsorship very successfully, and I hope we gave them a good return for their generous support. I am sure their partnerships with the Scottish Government improved for a while at least.

Over the years, with the help of a great team, Morag Reid, our Office Manager and Secretary to the Perth Hunt, deserves a special mention. Putting up with me needs huge patience and skill, but we worked well together and she was my right hand. A new stable block is now in place on the racecourse site, a dream of mine for many years. A new hotel, The Lodge, opened in June 2016 and plans to increase the office space have now been realised. The hotel should be a wonderful facility for visiting stable staff and should ensure more runners come to Perth racecourse on a regular basis. I am also sure the public will enjoy this quality accommodation at an affordable price in a unique setting for many years to come.

It has all been an awful lot of fun. Remarkably my head recovered enough to be useful at times and has never given me any more trouble, apart from the odd bout of concussion if I ever fell too hard on my bottom, but that has always been manageable, and I certainly knew how to handle it. How very fortunate I have been. I move on now to give all my energies into fighting another battle – my own cancer. Once I had digested the shock of being told I had between two and five years, the dreaded question all cancer patients have to ask, there was only one route for me and that was to carry on living life in the fast lane whenever I possibly could. I had shrugged off injuries in the past and I am shrugging off this one; I am determined to double my life expectancy. I am making my own body as fit as I can to fight this horrible disease. My faith helps me keep strong and I hope this will give me time to enjoy my grandchildren, Rory and Florence, and to catch a few more fish with my friends. I am glad I had my time race riding when I did. I certainly tried to make the most of it, but what mistakes I made along the way, not least ignoring concussion at almost every opportunity, and I certainly should also have sat still on some of the wonderful horses I rode and not just kicked and kicked. Perth racecourse and I fitted like a glove and we got together at the perfect time. If you have not been racing there I hope you can find the time to enjoy all that this little jewel has to offer.

Index

Photographic Acknowledgements
Plate Section

Cranhamphoto: page 5
Fraser Band: page 7 middle
Kenneth Bright: page 4 top
John Grossick: page 7 bottom
James Harrigan: page 2 bottom
Alec Russell: page 3 top
Bernard Parkin: pages 6 bottom, 7 top